How to Read an English Garden

How to Read an English Garden

Andrew Eburne &

Richard Taylor

EBURY
PRESS

A M D G
for Africa and Aurelia, Isobel and Mary

First published in Great Britain in 2006

Text © Andrew Eburne and Richard Taylor 2006
See page 272 for details of photographs and illustrations

The *How to Read* series is based on an original idea by Richard Taylor.

First published by Ebury Press
Random House, 20 Vauxhall Bridge Road, London SW1V 2SA
Random House Australia (Pty) Limited
20 Alfred Street, Milsons Point, Sydney, New South Wales 2061, Australia
Random House New Zealand Limited
18 Poland Road, Glenfield, Auckland 10, New Zealand
Random House South Africa (Pty) Limited
Endulini, 5A Jubilee Road, Parktown 2193, South Africa

The Random House Group Limited Reg. No. 954009
www.randomhouse.co.uk

A CIP catalogue record for this book is available from the British Library.

Editor: Patricia Burgess
Series editor: Richard Taylor
Designer: David Fordham

ISBN 0 091 90900 7
(ISBN 9780091909000 from January 2007)

Papers used by Ebury Press are natural, recyclable products
made from wood grown in sustainable forests.

Printed by Tien Wah Press in Singapore

PREVIOUS PAGE: *Islamic
influence shines through the
exotic Regency gardens of
Sezincote, Gloucestershire.*

RIGHT: *The terraces of Dartington
Hall, Devon, have their regular
lines surreally emphasised by the
early morning frost.*

CONTENTS

1. Cerastium tomentosum.
2. Alternanthera amœna.
3. Pyrethrum Golden Feather.
4. Mesembryanthemum cordifolium variegatum.
5. Alternanthera magnifica.
6. Echeveria secunda glauca.

ABOVE: *A geometric Victorian carpet bedding scheme, using summer-flowering annuals.*

8

PREFACE

THE INSPIRATION FOR this book came to Richard Taylor in the wake of the overwhelming response to his *How to Read a Church*, published in 2003. Gardens and parks are among the most popular visitor attractions in the UK today: it's estimated that over 15 million of us will make such a visit this year. Yet for the growing band of garden visitors there is only limited guidance as to what they will find in the course of their visit and how they might understand it. There are many academic studies of garden history and a number of popular accounts, but between these books on the one hand, and the various leaflets and guides sold by the gardens themselves on the other, there seemed a gap. Richard's inspiration was to supply that missing piece of the garden lover's jigsaw by writing a book that explains each of the many elements that make up the historic garden and how they got there. To help him he turned to one of his oldest friends, Andrew Eburne. Andrew is a garden historian and consultant, but twenty years ago he and Richard lived on opposite sides of the same staircase as they studied English together at Oxford. Together they planned the book that follows. The writing itself has been Andrew's responsibility, but Richard's advice and counsel, and his comments on and suggestions for each completed chapter, have been an essential and invaluable part of that process. The result, they hope, is a book that adds something to what Francis Bacon called 'the purest of human pleasures': the garden.

OVERLEAF: *Vivid high-Victorian bedding, recently restored at Waddesdon Manor, Buckinghamshire.*

Introduction
READING A GARDEN

Show me your garden...and I will tell you what you are like
ALFRED AUSTIN

How do you go about 'reading' a garden? For Francis Bacon (1561–1626), a garden was famously 'the purest of human pleasures'; for many of us today a garden is simply there to be enjoyed. Human beings have been gardening for 4000 years, however, and behind even the simplest domestic garden there lie centuries of imagination, exploration and experimentation. This book describes and explains each of the many elements that combine to create the modern or historic garden: from lawns to lilies, from vegetables to vineyards, from canals to cascades. Understanding these elements – the role they play within gardens, and how they came into existence – can make even that purest of pleasures still richer and more complete.

This is not intended to be a book about garden history: there are specialist works on that subject, and some of these are listed in the suggestions for further reading (see page 261). But we will draw widely on garden history – partly because so many of the gardens open to visitors have a special historic quality or condition, and partly because events in garden history can have consequences for the most basic constituents of our own gardens. If, for example, an ambitious Scottish nurseryman, Charles Lawson, had not introduced Italian rye grass to Britain in 1833, and the Lawson's cypress from California in 1854, our lawns and hedges

LEFT: *The eighteenth-century harmony of water, wood and stone in the gardens of Studley Royal, Yorkshire.*

would look very different today. Lawson was trying to break traditions, and went bankrupt in the effort, but he changed the ordinary domestic garden for ever. When we consider the role played by the lawn in front of a great country house, or in our own back garden, the stories of people such as Charles Lawson will inevitably inform our reading. History – described 2000 years ago as *lux veritatis* (the light of truth) – is our own, indispensable reading-light.

GARDEN CREATION

GARDENS ARE THE consequence of a meeting between human beings and the natural organic world around them. Their basic requirements are simple. Water, whether natural or irrigated. Light. A growing medium – which can be soil, or a pool of water. Protection from extremes of temperature or wind, if necessary: walls, fences or hedges. And a means for us to experience and enjoy the garden: paths and seats. Probably the first successful attempt to meet those requirements was made in the temple gardens of the Fertile Crescent of the Middle East (a strip of land comprising the lower Nile Valley, the eastern Mediterranean coast, Syria and Mesopotamia) some 4000 years ago – though even today some gardeners (including the present writers) will struggle to do so. Over many centuries, however, the creation of gardens has been marked by ever-increasing diversity, sophistication and elaboration. Those developments, and the traces they have left behind them, will be explored in the chapters that follow. First and foremost, though, gardens are created places. Inevitably they reflect our feelings about ourselves, our place in the world, even our intellectual identity; it is perhaps no coincidence that so many of the walls and enclosures that characterized pre-Reformation gardens were demolished in the eighteenth century to create the unbounded gardens of a restless Enlightenment. To read a garden is to read a story of historic human interest.

GARDENS & CHANGE

GARDENS NEVER STAND STILL. This is a truth known to anyone who has ever wielded a spade or trowel: if this year you don't do your weeding, next year the garden will be unrecognizable. But it's also true on a much larger scale, and those changes make our task as garden investigators both more difficult and more fascinating.

ABOVE: *The garden's vulnerability to change and decay has often been explored symbolically, as this Renaissance woodcut of Death in the garden shows.*

The earliest gardens in history were adjuncts to temples or palaces, and it remains the case that most historic and, indeed, domestic gardens were laid out for the first time when the house beside them was built. Gardens, however, are more vulnerable to neglect than buildings. A neglected building may stand for a century, but a neglected garden will vanish far sooner.

Gardens, too, get changed more radically than buildings: they are after all both cheaper and easier to change. When, for example, Robert Walpole (1676–1745), Britain's first prime minister, built his great house at Houghton in Norfolk in the early eighteenth century, he spent about £22,000 on the building, and £900 on the gardens (the equivalent of £2.8 million, and £110,000 today). It was the most expensive house in the country, and inevitably it prompted a lot of envy. When one of Walpole's less well-off neighbours, John Hobart, wished to improve his house, he couldn't afford to change the building – fortunately for us, as it was and remains a fine Jacobean mansion. Instead, he ripped out almost every trace of the original gardens and replaced them with a modish, bare layout. Of course, great houses experience changes too: some are given new façades or new wings; some are rebuilt entirely. But generally speaking, gardens have experienced more change, and of a more profound nature, than the buildings they were born with – through neglect, or deliberate redevelopment, or a combination of the two.

What are the consequences of this? Historic gardens are a patchwork. It is very rare that a garden is entirely razed and begun again from scratch; there are always survivals from an earlier layout – forgotten corners, plants or trees. Even John Hobart overlooked some walls and trees from the previous century. Other gardens experience instead a cycle of neglect and

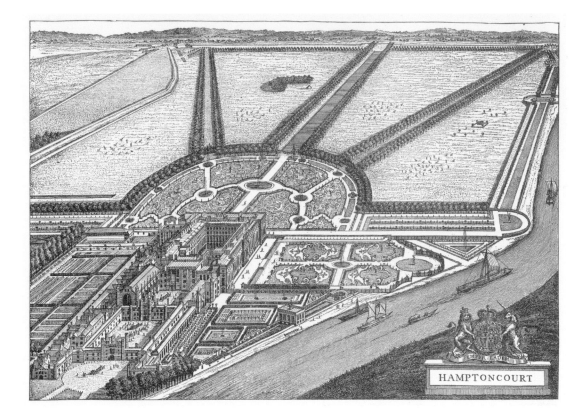

ABOVE: *A bird's eye view of Hampton Court, drawn by Johannes Kipp in the early 18th century and showing the lavish formal gardens created by William and Mary.*

renewal; whilst for many historic gardens – including some of the most famous – redevelopment is more a process of accretion: different bits added on by different owners and designers in different ages. The gardens at Stowe in Buckinghamshire are a good example. First laid out in the late seventeenth century, they have substantial additions made by Charles Bridgeman in the 1720s, by William Kent in the 1730s, and by Lancelot 'Capability' Brown in the 1750s – and the work of all three designers was modified in succeeding centuries. We call Stowe an eighteenth-century garden, but a visitor in 1725 would have seen a garden completely different from the one on view in 1750, and completely different again from the one in 1800, let alone in 2000. Most historic gardens, then, represent a palimpsest of different historic periods. This makes every garden unique, and it also makes it harder to read. To do so successfully is to recognize the role that different elements of different ages play in the unique character of the whole.

✜ GARDENS & SPACE

IT IS WORTH NOTING that gardens also reflect attitudes to space, and that these too change over time. Medieval flower gardens were enclosed and small – often very small by modern standards – while eighteenth-century gardens were expansive and open. The re-creation of Queen Eleanor's thirteenth-century garden (or herber) that you can see today at Winchester Castle in Hampshire measures a modest 30 x 90 feet (9 x 27 m). Queen Anne's eighteenth-century garden at Hampton Court in Surrey, on the other hand, covered 74 acres (30 hectares). This is not because Queen Anne had more money – she was actually rather hard up – but because the idea of a private garden and the space allocated to it had expanded enormously in the intervening 500 years.

Of course, medieval landowners had their parks, too – usually for raising and hunting deer. But these were very much private affairs, often with high walls – and when it came to the smaller flower gardens near a grand house, privacy again seems to have been high on the list of desired attributes. Arbours that could not be seen into, seats that were not overlooked, hedges that kept the outside world at bay…these elements appear frequently in garden descriptions from the period. Indeed, the medieval flower garden was often called *hortus conclusus* – a garden that is enclosed, confined, or shut up. In one sense, these spaces are alien to us; in another, they have proved remarkably resilient. Twentieth-century gardens are often arranged as a series of 'rooms' divided by walls or high hedges: the gardens at Sissinghurst in Kent and at Hidcote in Gloucestershire are good examples of these. They were inspired by the Anglo-Italian fashions of the early twentieth century, which revived the gardens of the Italian Renaissance, and the tradition of the *giardino segreto* (secret garden). The *giardino segreto* was itself a direct descendant of the *hortus conclusus*. When we enjoy the separateness of a garden 'room', its almost magical creation of its own world and atmosphere, we share a pleasure with the medieval gardeners of 700 years ago.

During the eighteenth century these priorities were to a considerable extent reversed. Enclosures were thrown down, walls demolished, hedges grubbed up. The familiar image of the country house marooned in acres of lawn dates from this period. One of the most important practical contributions to this isolation was the invention of the ha-ha. A ha-ha is essentially an invisible wall: a wall (sometimes a fence or hedge) built inside a ditch so that you can't see it until you are very near. The word 'ha-ha', originally French, derives from the exclamation of

RIGHT: *The Privy Garden
at Hampton Court,
restored to its late-17th-
century condition in
1995.*

surprise made by the visitor on discovering this barrier (or perhaps on falling into it). The practical consequence of the ha-ha was two-fold: it meant that you could keep livestock away from the house, but enjoy views from the house without the interruption of walls or fences. For the first time the garden could seem a continuous part of the parkland or farmland beyond. So it was said of the revolutionary eighteenth-century designer William Kent, 'he leapt the fence, and saw that all Nature was a Garden'. When all nature is your garden, the possibilities are literally infinite. Our sense of space is crucial to our sense of what is possible in a garden.

THE EXPERIENCE OF GARDENS

IN A WAY THIS BOOK is all about the experience of gardens, and how the quality of that experience can be improved by our knowledge and understanding of what gardens contain. But it's also worth considering the way in which we experience gardens. A single example will suffice. Almost every garden, however large or small, will possess in it somewhere a seat. Where that seat is located may have something to do with the plants nearby, especially if they are scented. It may, if the owner is fond of sun-bathing, have to do with the amount of sunshine available – or, if not, with the amount of shade. Almost invariably, however, a garden seat will be placed to provide us with something to look at. But the idea itself – of experiencing the garden as 'something to look at' – has a quite limited and specific history.

We think of gardens, parkland and countryside as types of landscape; we call the professionals responsible for the design of green spaces 'landscape architects'. But 'landscape' is a painting term: it comes from the Dutch word *landskip*, which was borrowed by the English of Shakespeare's time to describe a kind of picture. It was only in the early eighteenth century that 'landskip' began to be applied to the natural, physical world, and inevitably it suggests a very particular way of looking at gardens and parks. The poet and gardener William Shenstone (1714–63) coined the term 'landscape gardener' because he thought that gardens ought to be designed by landscape painters. The guide to Shenstone's garden, The Leasowes (Warwickshire), instructed visitors to see the garden as a sequence of 'landskips', 'pictures' and 'sketches'. This was the beginning of what came to be known as the 'picturesque movement'. It turned gardens and parks into very static things: the best garden is just like a picture. A special looking-glass could be purchased, called a 'Claude glass', after the neo-

BELOW: *The geometric forms of the 17th-century garden are not always sympathetic for modern gardeners. But these Oxford gardens show how much variety of shape and planting could be achieved within a small area.*

INTRODUCTION:
READING A
GARDEN
✺

classical painter Claude Lorrain (1600–82). It consisted of a rather gloomy oval mirror: so that instead of looking at the real garden, you looked at its reflection in the mirror – and saw the muted, framed colours of an Old Master. And if the gardens were static, so in a way were the visitors: passive spectators, confined to a numbered sequence of views – often not even moving to the next viewpoint by themselves, but transported in sedan chairs or carriages. A garden experienced without effort.

One curious consequence of this is that in the larger eighteenth-century landscape gardens we are often at the wrong height to appreciate exactly what is going on. The grounds were designed so that the very best views were available from the perspective of a visitor seated in a carriage: a metre or so lower, on foot, and sometimes the effect is lost. By the close of the nineteenth century, however, fashion had turned to more untamed spaces – so-called 'wild gardens': not landscapes to gaze upon passively, but wildernesses to lose yourself in. Some of today's favoured garden features – the wildflower meadow, for example – date from that period.

The underlying relationship, however, remains the same: different types of garden provide a different kind of experience for their visitors – and sometimes even impose one. But garden-makers and visitors still preserve their own expectations, their own sense of what constitutes the perfect or proper garden – and, if you like, a dialogue between each other. And all these will help determine the final experience.

ABOVE: *William Robinson's garden at Gravetye Manor, Sussex, showing the interplay between natural planting and formal stonework.*

GARDENS & NATURE

GARDENS, AS WE have noted, are the outcome of a meeting between human beings and the natural world. But just how natural, or unnatural, is that outcome? The question may seem academic, yet it has shaped the way people have seen and created their gardens for almost 300 years. The development of the English landscape garden was due in part to a desire to see gardens as paintings. Ironically, it was also driven by a desire for gardens to be more natural – or perhaps more like the exquisite scenes of nature depicted by landscape painters. The essayist Joseph Addison, who in 1712 urged his readers to turn their gardens into 'landskips', declared in the same paragraph that 'there is generally in Nature something more Grand and August, than what we meet with in the Curiosities of Art'. Addison described his own garden as 'a natural Wilderness', with flowers growing 'in the greatest Luxuriancy and Profusion', trees in

BELOW: *The gardens at Hestercombe, Somerset, were designed by Edwin Lutyens and Gertrude Jekyll. Lutyens' strong architectural lines are softened by Jekyll's planting.*

INTRODUCTION:
READING A
GARDEN
❋

'as great a Wildness as their Natures will permit', and a stream running 'in the same manner as it would do in an open Field'. In fact, Addison's garden was rather more strait-laced than this, but the terms of the debate had been set. Out went 'unnatural' formality, symmetry and straight lines. In came 'natural' informality, assymetry and 'serpentines'. As William Kent is reported to have said, 'Nature abhors a straight line'. This has become a well-established means of describing gardens: the gardens of the Elizabethans, and of the seventeenth century, are formal; the English landscape garden of the eighteenth century is informal. Gardens such as those created in the early twentieth century by Edwin Lutyens and Gertrude Jekyll (Hestercombe in Somerset, for example) are a mixture of the two – strict architectural lines softened by luxuriant planting. Of course, the debate itself did not stand still. In the later eighteenth century the

landscape gardens designed by Capability Brown in the 'natural', informal tradition came to be seen by some as being overly manicured – having too much 'smoothness' about them – and were therefore condemned as unnatural. The natural preference turned instead towards 'roughness' – and so the debate rumbled on.

The great advocate of roughness in gardens was Sir Uvedale Price (1747–1829), who lived in the suitably rugged Welsh borders. Price was ferocious in argument, but had thought deeply about landscape. His conclusion was that a house and garden required a kind of gradation between what was artificial and what was natural. The house was the most artificial, and stood at the centre of the landscape. Then came the formal gardens, still relatively artificial; then more informal gardens; then parkland, which was very like 'natural' landscape; and finally the open countryside beyond.

Ironically for a man writing from the heart of Romanticism, Price's idea resurrected one of the great precepts of the Renaissance: that the garden should be an extension of the architecture of the house. His model does not of course apply to every garden, but it was very influential, and something like this gradation between the natural and the artificial can be seen in many historic gardens today.

❖ GARDENS & SOCIETY

IN READING A GARDEN we should always be aware of its social and political context. Indeed, those contexts are sometimes difficult to ignore. When the 1st Duke of Beaufort drove an avenue of beech trees in a straight line 2½ miles (4 km) from his front door, his decision was in part aesthetic, but it was also undoubtedly political – the ultimate statement of power and ownership for a man who, in the late seventeenth century, ruled Gloucestershire as his own personal kingdom (you can still see the avenue today). Similarly, when Lord Cobham in 1732 was outmanoeuvred in government by the brilliant and unscrupulous Robert Walpole, he retired to his gardens at Stowe and promptly filled them with buildings and statues satirizing his political opponents and their ideology. The Temple of Ancient Virtue depicted those figures from the past to whom Cobham and his political allies looked for inspiration; the nearby Temple of Modern Virtue was built as a ruin containing a single mutilated torso in contemporary dress – perhaps a portrait of Walpole himself.

RIGHT: *The Temple of British Worthies at Stowe,
Buckinghamshire, is one of the most overtly political
garden buildings, celebrating sixteen 'Worthies' from
British history admired by Lord Cobham's Whig party.*

More generally, it's true that – until very recently – the gardens we visit have tended to be the gardens of the historic upper classes. The temptation is therefore to see gardens as the preserve of the upper classes, functioning primarily as a kind of status symbol. It's an attractive theory, but it has its limitations. To take just one example: as we've seen, the first ornamental gardens were almost certainly adjuncts of temples rather than private houses, created for spiritual reasons as much as temporal ones. This reminds us that the impulses behind garden creation are not simply those of social status, but are both more complex and more profound, having to do with our relationship with the natural world, with our sense of self, and with our sense of space and its value – alongside more narrow and easily defined factors, such as the desire to impress our neighbours. It's also worth noting that visiting gardens has been a favoured occupation of those with leisure for many centuries, and that those with leisure today can scarcely be divided by class. During the eighteenth century a visit to the gardens of the elite might well have been restricted to 'persons of quality' (though there were notable exceptions). By contrast, at the start of the twenty-first century one of the most visited gardens in England is Cornwall's Eden Project – a re-creation, in vast greenhouses called 'biospheres', of different climates and flora from around the world. This is gardening not as an aristocratic plaything, but as an educational enterprise; financed not by inherited millions, but by a charitable trust. Finally, we should remember that garden-making itself has always been a democratic occupation, and that in the modern age the gardens of the historic middle and working classes are of increasing interest to visitors and historians alike.

One case in which social concerns rightly predominate is in the role played by women. There have always been rich, usually aristocratic males creating gardens of exceptional importance, whether it be Lord Lumley in the sixteenth century or Lord Cobham in the eighteenth. But the historical baseline running quietly and continuously behind these spectacular achievements is one of a traditional division of labour, difficult to understand for us but commonplace in its own day: men tend the orchards and their fruit, while women tend the flower and kitchen garden. As Thomas Tusser (*c.*1524–1580) wrote in one of the very earliest English gardening books, *Wife, unto thy garden!* It is still possible to see areas called 'My Lady's Garden' in grounds laid out during the eighteenth or nineteenth century, and some of the finest historic flower gardens in England owe their existence to women.

A BRIEF HISTORY OF ENGLISH GARDEN DESIGN

IT IS SCARCELY POSSIBLE within the confines of this book to do justice to the variety of English garden design and to the achievement of English garden designers over the past 500 years and more. However, as the names of certain designers and of certain periods in the history of gardens will recur in the pages that follow, we offer here a brief summary of the principal influences.

ROMAN GARDENS

THE BEST EXAMPLES of Roman gardens visible today are to be found around the shores of the Mediterranean (there are some fine remains in North Africa). They are rare in England, though the Roman villa at Fishbourne in Sussex has a re-created garden. Of course, a 'Roman garden' could occur just about anywhere in Europe across a period of up to 500 years, so we should be wary of generalizations. That said, Roman gardens can be broadly divided into the enclosed, formal city gardens, and the more open and informal villa gardens of the countryside. Examples of the former include the many peristyle gardens of Pompeii and Herculaneum. A peristyle is a covered colonnade (rather like a cloister) running round the garden, and

these smaller city gardens would be designed in straight lines, with statues and wall-paintings, and water in ponds, fountains and bird-baths. Larger gardens can be seen at imperial villas such as that at Tivoli, near Rome, or in the villas of provincial governors, such as Pliny the Younger (*c.* 61– *c.* 115) (e.g. Tusculum near Frascati). Very little of this type of gardening can be seen today in England, but its influence is everywhere. Medieval gardens, including the *hortus conclusus*, draw deeply on Roman models, while the rediscovery of Roman villa gardens, and the descriptions found in Pliny's letters, drove garden fashions in the early eighteenth century.

MEDIEVAL GARDENS

NO ORIGINAL MEDIEVAL GARDEN survives, though several have been re-created in England and elsewhere in Europe. Our knowledge of medieval gardens really begins three centuries after the fall of the Roman Empire, with the rise of Charlemagne in the eighth century. Several garden types have been identified: the kitchen garden; the physic garden for medicinal herbs; the herber or enclosed flower garden; the orchard – used primarily

LEFT: A 16th-century woodcut showing a geometric garden with a covered arbour and a trellised balustrade surrounding the central bed.

for relaxation, not food; the deer park; and the landscape park, or pleasance. Vineyards were also commonly planted, especially by monasteries. Although the total number of known plant species was very small – perhaps 300 – the range of plants grown might surprise a modern gardener: the two centuries after the Norman invasion (1066) were among the warmest in England's recorded history, and until the weather cooled around 1400, many plants later confined to more southerly climes could be grown in English (and Scottish) gardens.

TUDOR & ELIZABETHAN GARDENS

TUDOR GARDENS WERE designed to be seen first from above, from the upper floor of the house. They were laid out formally, in squares ornamented by knots (see pages 74–8). Henry VIII's garden at Hampton Court was described as 'so enknotted it cannot be expressed'. Within the garden, mounds of earth called 'mounts' also provided raised viewing areas. Walks were often covered; mazes were popular; and a peculiar feature of the largest gardens was a profusion of painted wooden heraldic devices on poles. A re-creation of a Tudor garden may be seen at the Tudor House Museum in Southampton.

The relative prosperity of the late sixteenth century funded the building of

RIGHT: Another 16th-century garden being watered with a hydraulic pump. Note the balustrading again, and the covered bee-skeps in the corner.

many new manor houses, as well as the first generation of plant-collectors (see page 38). To the basic model of the Tudor garden the Elizabethans began to add more elaborate banqueting houses, topiary, grottoes and water features. They were also keen kitchen-gardeners, and the first guides to husbandry were published during this period.

SEVENTEENTH-CENTURY GARDENS

THE PROFLIGATE JACOBEAN court was responsible for the building of some extraordinary houses and gardens, including those at Hatfield in Hertfordshire and Blickling in Norfolk. This spending, combined with a period of relative peace in Europe, lured international designers to

ABOVE: *This princely layout of 1601 shows the extravagance of contemporary gardens, with arbours built on a monumental scale surrounding an elaborate fountain.*

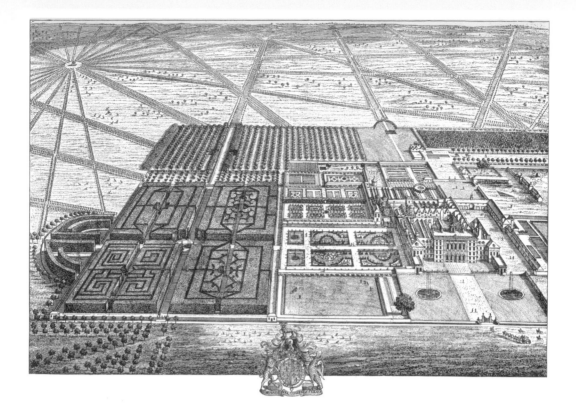

England. Two notable features – of the grandest sites at least – were a new 'design unity' of house and garden, inspired by Continental models, and the use of elaborate water features, such as fountains and even automata (moving statues powered by hydraulics). This period also saw the first botanic garden in England, created at Oxford in 1621. (There had been earlier examples in Italy, but the very earliest were probably the creation of the Arab world.)

The English Civil Wars (1642–51) saw the destruction of many fine gardens, including the royal gardens at Wimbledon in London and Theobalds (pronounced 'tibbalds') in Hertfordshire – though the Puritans had their own interest in plants, and developed more productive kitchen gardens. Following his years of exile in France, the restoration of Charles II in 1660 brought a powerful renewal of French influence in gardens. His return coincided with that of the French royal gardener André Mollet (see page 36), who had designed gardens for Charles's mother, Henrietta Maria, twenty years earlier. High fashion in gardens was driven by the court: the French style was inevitably modified by the accession of William of Orange in 1692, and by the Dutch fondness for sequences of square parterres (see pages 129–31) set each side of a strong central axis. Outside court circles, however, change was more gradual, and houses belonging to the gentry usually retained their less regimented (though still formal) layouts of earlier years.

RIGHT: *Plas Newydd, Anglesey, was laid out in the late 18th century with advice from Humphrey Repton to make the most of its dramatically picturesque location.*

EIGHTEENTH-CENTURY GARDENS

THE GREAT CHANGE in our gardens, as we have already noted, came with the eighteenth-century English landscape garden. This period witnessed a veritable explosion of garden-making, and its design features are difficult to summarize briefly, but they include planting that is informal and irregular, rather than formal and regular; the creation of (often large) irregularly shaped lakes, as opposed to geometric canals; the use of curved rather than straight lines; the destruction of walls and enclosures, and the opening up of views; the use of the ha-ha to unite gardens and parkland; large expanses of turf for riding, carriage-driving and grazing; the construction of eye-catching, iconographic garden buildings, such as temples and obelisks; and the creation of

ABOVE: *The gardens at Stowe, Buckinghamshire, exemplify the 18th-century delight in informal landscaping as opposed to the linear and geometric gardens of the previous century.*

long, winding drives to pass all around the boundaries of the landscape. Capability Brown (see page 37) and his imitators were responsible for the transformation along these lines of literally thousands of English estates during the mid-eighteenth century. By the end of the century, however, a backlash of sorts was visible in the 'picturesque' preference for a more rugged landscape of ruins and rough trees.

NINETEENTH-CENTURY GARDENS

REGENCY GARDENERS DEVELOPED a new interest in the diversity of plant life, particularly flowers, reflected in the creation of the Royal Horticultural Society (1804). The energetic and eclectic Victorians for their part began to explore a range of garden styles, with no single model predominating. They were interested in garden history – not so much in an academic sense, as in a more carefree, pick-your-own fashion, which saw the widespread use of 'Italianate' and 'French' formal designs, ostensibly paying homage to the sixteenth and seventeenth centuries, but with an unmistakable modern twist. Where the Victorians excelled was, of course, technology: greenhouses and hothouses were far larger, and far hotter, than ever before. This allowed the cultivation of many more exotic plants, which could be protected under glass through the English winter, then let loose with all their fiery colours in the summer. The bright massed 'carpet beds' that still adorn some public parks might be found in any Victorian garden that could afford the winter fuel and the great number of gardeners necessary to maintain them. By way of contrast, the Arts and Crafts movement of the late nineteenth and early twentieth centuries was inspired by John Ruskin (1819–1900) and William Morris (1834–96) to encourage traditional craftsmanship and materials in houses and gardens. Broadly (though not exclusively) middle class, it revived the cottage garden and the cultivation of old-fashioned flowers.

TWENTIETH-CENTURY GARDENS

IT IS SCARCELY POSSIBLE to describe a single twentieth-century style in gardens. One of the most significant features of the period, however, was the loss of a great many large gardens. Three factors played an important part in their demise. First, agricultural depression at the start of the century meant that many country estates were no longer self-sufficient. Second, garden labour was both scarcer and more expensive (a consequence in part of World War I), so gardens were more expensive to maintain and there was less money to do so. Third, death duties (introduced in 1894) meant that landowners could no longer afford to pass property on to their children, so hundreds of country houses were sold or demolished and their gardens lost. The National Trust did step in to save some gardens (Hidcote is a notable example), and garden history acquired a new popularity. Garden design in the twentieth century was as eclectic as that in the preceding century: the early decades in particular saw some Anglo-Italian and Arts and Crafts masterpieces – Iford in Wiltshire, Hidcote, Sissinghurst and Hestercombe. In the later decades of the century, historic revivals and restorations increased dramatically in both number and accuracy; indeed, all four of the gardens just mentioned have been restored. Meanwhile, garden designers, like other artists, began to use an extraordinary variety of new materials: glass, steel, concrete, plastic and aluminium. But perhaps the greatest achievement of the century was to legitimize the small garden. For the first time authorities on gardening began to treat what happened in the everyday garden as having an interest all its own.

⊞ ENGLISH GARDEN DESIGNERS

PERHAPS WE SHOULD SAY rather 'designers of gardens in England', since the earliest celebrated ones were almost always foreign, and usually French. Below, in chronological order, are the most influential.

ANDRE MOLLET

THE FIRST TO LEAVE a mark of nationwide significance was André Mollet (died *c.* 1665), a designer with a pan-European clientele. He designed gardens for Charles I at St James's Palace and at Wimbledon, before returning after the Restoration to create St James's Park for Charles II. His work is marked by long avenues of trees (usually lime or elm), long canals (St James's Park originally had a canal running its entire length), *parterres de broderie* (swirling designs of box set against a background of coloured sand or earth), and *bosquets* (groves of trees cut through by walks).

CHARLES BRIDGEMAN

ANOTHER ROYAL GARDENER, an Englishman this time, Charles Bridgeman (*c.* 1690–1738) came to prominence in the early eighteenth century. He was responsible for the Royal Parks, including Hampton Court, Windsor and Hyde Park, and Kensington Gardens, where he designed the Serpentine lake. But arguably his best work was reserved for private aristocratic clients – Lord Cobham at Stowe and the Duke of Newcastle at Claremont in Surrey. He inherited the formality of the seventeenth century, and began to develop the informality of the eighteenth: he planted straight avenues and square parterres, but extended the planting of wide lawns and irregular woodland, and was the first designer to make repeated use of the ha-ha to open up the landscape.

WILLIAM KENT

A FAILED ARTIST, William Kent (1685–1748) brilliantly transcended his mediocre painting skills to create gardens and landscapes of astonishing invention. He was 'discovered' in Rome by Lord Burlington, who brought Kent back to help with the gardens at Chiswick in west London. After the Prince of Wales asked Kent to design the gardens at Carlton House in The Mall, the Kentian style – based in part on the ideal landscapes painted by Claude and Nicolas Poussin (1594–1665) – became the height of fashion. His achievement was to re-create the ideal landscape while making it appear the work of nature. He worked on relatively few gardens – they include Stowe and Holkham (Norfolk) – but his influence was enormous.

LANCELOT 'CAPABILITY' BROWN

CAPABILITY BROWN (1716–83) acquired his nickname through his diplomatic habit of referring to the 'capabilities' of the estates where he was employed. He 'improved' at least 200 landscapes, compared to about a dozen by his predecessor William Kent. Brown was efficient, professional and perhaps a little formulaic: his landscapes are characterized by large, undulating slopes of grass, often reaching up to the house-front; by the planting of trees in 'naturalistic' small clumps, or even singly; by the creation of a perimeter belt of trees around the estate, with a drive running through it; and by serpentine or irregularly shaped lakes. He was, above all, a brilliant engineer, adept at moving large quantities of both land and water. His skill netted him huge rewards: the Duke of Newcastle paid him £21,500 (about £2.5 million today) over ten years, and his annual turnover averaged £15,000 (nearly £2 million today).

HUMPHRY REPTON

HUMPHRY REPTON (1752–1818) proclaimed himself the successor to 'Capability' Brown in 1788, after earlier careers in business and farming had failed. For each landscape he worked on he created a Red Book – a text, usually bound in red leather, discussing the landscape in question and illustrating proposed changes with clever before-and-after watercolours on flaps of paper. His style was much influenced by Brown, and his proposals often modified existing work by his predecessor. Practically, however, he differed from Brown in two important respects: he did not undertake the work of 'improvement' himself, acting instead as a kind of design consultant; and he never made much money. He might charge a client £100 for a Red Book and a visit of a few weeks, unlike Brown, who could (and did) extend work over a number of years.

GERTRUDE JEKYLL & EDWIN LUTYENS

GERTRUDE JEKYLL (1843–1932) was another garden designer who was first a painter. Always troubled by poor eyesight, in her early fifties she was advised by her doctor to give up painting. Instead she turned to gardening, and (perhaps surprizingly) to writing. In 1889 she met the young architect Edwin Lutyens (1869–1944), who designed her house at Munstead Wood, near Guildford in Surrey, and together they shared a twenty-year partnership, working on some seventy gardens. Their style was characterized by the Arts and Crafts love of traditional materials and working methods, and an organic completeness of design. In particular, Lutyens' firm architectural lines and vistas were complemented by Jekyll's extraordinary grasp of colour and abundant planting. Their best work can be seen at Hestercombe; later they collaborated in creating cemeteries for the war dead.

PLANT COLLECTING & CULTIVATION

FROM ANCIENT TIMES through to the Renaissance, the chief vehicles for the movement of plants (other than their own natural mechanisms) were war and religion. Both the Romans and the Crusaders were responsible for plant introductions to England, while communication between monasteries spread plant knowledge and material across medieval Europe. Until the late sixteenth century, however, the number of plants available to an English gardener was relatively limited – a mere 300 species, compared to over 14,000 species and 70,000 cultivars today. The Elizabethans, with their access to new trade routes around the world, were the first great plant collectors. In 1577 William Harrison wrote of his amazement 'to see how manie strange hearbs, plants, and annuall fruits, are daily brought unto us from the Indies, Americas, Taprobane [Southeast Asia], Canarie Iles, and all parts of the World'. Plant introductions since that time have followed – and sometimes driven – Western European explorations of the wider world: from the Atlantic coast of the Americas in the sixteenth century, to the Himalayas in the 1920s, to jungle expeditions of the present day. The introduction of new species has dramatically changed the way we garden; it has made the garden a place of infinite possibility.

CHAPTER ONE

ARRIVING

An approach, which does not evidently lead to the house, or which does not take the shortest course, cannot be right.
HUMPHREY REPTON

THE INTRODUCTION HAS described various ways of approaching gardens and their meaning, both historically and philosophically. Now we turn to the physical routes – the drives, approaches and ridings. The way a garden is reached can tell us a good deal about it: how it is intended to be experienced and how old it is. Reading a garden can begin some distance before it is actually reached.

DRIVES

THE DRIVE, OR DRIVEWAY, of a modern house may be simply the piece of land between the house and the street, sometimes no longer than the car parked on it. On a country estate it may be measured not in feet but in miles. There are drives that go straight to the house and drives that go nowhere near it; and there are those, like the one at Blaise Castle near Bristol, that do go to the house, but make every possible diversion along the way. All these drives have a common though divided ancestry.

The drive as a route to the house is a Georgian invention. Originally, 'driving' was what you did to animals – either to sheep and other farm stock, or (more rarely) to deer when hunting.

LEFT: *The Oxford Bridge at Stowe, Buckinghamshire, formed part of the grand approach to the estate created by Earl Temple in 1761.*

RIGHT: *A bluebell-lined drive at Nanhoron,
Gwynedd.*

(It was also what the devil did to people when, hunting their souls, he made them lustful: 'he needs must go that the devil drives'.) In the seventeenth century, as wheeled transport increased, it came also to apply to coaches and carriages: a coachman didn't just drive the horses, he drove the vehicle itself. Early coaches were notoriously uncomfortable: Queen Elizabeth I, for example, who thought nothing of a 10-mile (16-km) ride on horseback, found the jolting of her coach made her physically ill. The eighteenth century, however, saw improvements in carriage design, road laying and horse breeding. For the first time, driving had become a potentially relaxing and pleasant experience. More specifically, it was a pleasant way to experience landscape. We have seen how a designed landscape could be construed as a sequence of views; what more relaxing way of taking in those views than from the comfort of a well-sprung carriage? And if the route from the high road to the house took in some of those views on the way, so much the better. Around 1800, then, there was a surge in demand both for carriages and for routes – especially those with good views – that a carriage might drive down. So a verb became a noun and 'the drive' was born.

The great advocate of a drive with a view was Humphry Repton (see page 37), and it was he who designed the exceptionally long drive at Blaise Castle. Short drives leading straight to the house, and usually laid with gravel, became more common during the nineteenth century. Again, these were simply carriage-drives, and a consequence of the explosion in carriage ownership. It is difficult to overestimate the importance of that explosion. To give just one, international example: in the American city of Philadelphia carriage ownership increased by over 2000 per cent in the late eighteenth century – from thirty-nine carriages in 1761 to 827 in 1794 – and this was before the advances in suspension and tyre design of the 1820s. Among the practical consequences were the expansion of stables: more carriages meant more horses, which meant more smell and noise that you probably wanted to keep away from the house, which meant another road (or drive) had to be laid from the house to the stables. With more commercial traffic on the roads, there was more likelihood of tradesmen driving straight up to the front door. That, of course, would never do, so another feature of the nineteenth century was the laying of additional drives to take business visitors away from the house to the estate yard and offices.

The hunting sense of 'drive' persisted in a different way. Whereas the Elizabethans tended to describe the pursuit of animals as the 'chase' (and some open areas of forest still have that name, also given to modern streets located in former hunting parks), the Victorians resurrected

the word 'drive', particularly when coursing for hares or shooting birds, which are driven in a specific direction. To add to the confusion, in the late nineteenth century, when woodland gardens became fashionable again and a pleasure to drive through, the term 'drive' could apply to any cleared path through woodland that a carriage could be driven down. 'The Drive' was also the name given to a fashionable road in Hyde Park used for riding, and you may come across this in period accounts. As carriage driving became more popular, the routes devoted to it (and that still remain today on the outskirts of historic gardens) acquired a dizzying variety. The landscape gardener William Robinson complained in 1883: 'I went once to see the home of a poet of repute, and to get in was met by five different roads to find my way to the house.'

BELOW: *A drive cut through early 19th-century woodland at Old Sleningford, Yorkshire.*

APPROACHES

THE 'APPROACH' WAS the seventeenth-century equivalent of our modern drive – the way up to the house – but you are unlikely to find many described thus today. Again, it is a noun that has grown out of a verb, and dates from a time when people had begun both to travel more widely and to develop a more considered aesthetic sense of a house and its setting. In her journal of the 1680s, the intrepid traveller Celia Fiennes repeatedly describes the great houses she visited as 'very fine in ye approach'. During the eighteenth century, this

simple appreciation was overtaken by the fashion for sequential views and the more diverse experience of the English landscape park. Thomas Whately in his book *Observations on Modern Gardening* (1771) argued that the best way into a country house was 'a winding lateral approach', and used the estate at Caversham (Berkshire) with its wonderful mile-long approach as an example.

Blaise Castle has an approach as well as a drive, but the approach is the shorter of the two. Repton believed that the pendulum had swung too far in the direction of scenic meanderings, and that these should be the preserve of the drive, while the approach actually gets you to where you want to go: 'An approach, which does not evidently lead to the house, or which does not take the shortest course, cannot be right.' Repton had a great weakness for making definitions, and an even greater weakness for ignoring them. The approach at Blaise Castle hardly takes the shortest route to the house. It is much more like another of Repton's definitions of the approach, which 'passes through the most interesting part of the grounds, and will display the scenery of the place to the greatest advantage, without making any violent or unnecessary circuit, to include objects that do not naturally come within its reach'. In the nineteenth century, the approach was overtaken by the carriage-drive and its many variations.

RIDINGS

UNLIKE DRIVES AND APPROACHES, ridings do not typically constitute a main route to the house. You are more likely to see them in the wider parkland (though they may converge upon the house as the focal point of the park). They are simply extended grassy clearings in woodland, measuring between 20 and 60 feet (6 and 18 m) in width, although some can reach 300 feet (90 m); and up to 1 mile (1.6 km) in length. They may either join to form a circuit, or terminate on some viewpoint or object of interest. They are usually straight; if curved, they will date from after 1750, when serpentine lines started to become fashionable.

The history of ridings is closely bound up with that of hunting. As their name suggests, they are 'routes that you ride in': cleared ways for recreation on horseback. (The name, by the way, has nothing to do with the Ridings of Yorkshire or Canada; those come from the Anglo-Saxon word *thriding*, meaning 'a third'.) Long before the invention of carriages,

RIGHT: *The woodland walk at Little Bowden,
Berkshire. Despite the shade cast by the trees, this
garden is alive with colour from spring bulbs and
flowering trees such as magnolia.*

hunting was the chief form of recreation on horseback. The earliest ridings were probably Elizabethan, though it's possible they have an older medieval heritage. The courtier Sir Philip Sidney (1554–86) describes ridings around a lodge in his romance, the *Arcadia*: 'The Lodge is…built in the forme of a starre, having round about a garden framed into like points; and beyond the garden ridings cut out, each answering the angles of the Lodge.' This description tallies with contemporary accounts of Elizabethan hunting, in which stags might be pursued past the viewing platform of a hunting lodge, or past a 'stand', a platform from which the animal could be shot by crossbow or bow and arrow. Architect John James wrote in 1712 of woods that had 'no rolled Walks in them, only Ridings cut for Hunting', reminding us again that in the eighteenth-century hierarchy of parkland pleasures, walking came a distinct second place to galloping after animals. James was, after all, writing in the reign of one of the great hunting monarchs, Queen Anne, who had ridings, or 'rides' as they were sometimes abbreviated, cut in Hampton Court Park and Windsor Great Park. Anne grew too large to ride on horseback comfortably, and instead had a two-wheeled carriage specially designed for her. When the poet Jonathan Swift (1667–1745) visited her at Hampton Court in 1711 he reported that 'she hunts in a chaise with one horse, which she drives herself, and drives furiously, like Jehu, and is a mighty hunter, like Nimrod'. Nothing kept Anne from hunting, as Swift found: later in his visit he recorded that 'the Queen was hunting the stag till four this afternoon, and she drove in her chaise above forty miles, and it was five before we went to dinner'.

These hunting ridings were in use throughout the eighteenth and nineteenth centuries. The ubiquitous Humphry Repton observed one at Hanslope, in Buckinghamshire: 'the strait Glade or riding cut in the wood'. Almost inevitably, however, the development of the English landscape garden – in particular its blurring of the division between park and garden – led to some modification. Thomas Whately argued that when gardening we should think not just of a garden itself, but of 'a park, farm or a riding'. Hunting routes were now to be embellished with shrubs and decorative planting. Ridings might even be used as ways to sample the different views and aesthetic pleasures of the estate, without hunting anything at all; and, indeed, in the nineteenth century (despite the continued popularity of hunting), 'riding' and 'ride' came to apply to just about any path or track that you could ride down. Even Hyde Park had its ride, where fashionable society might show off. 'The Ride' was another name for

Left: *The Corinthian Arch at Stowe, Buckinghamshire, designed in 1765 to announce to visitors that they had arrived on the estate – and to provide an eyecatcher when viewed from the house.*

CHAPTER ONE:
ARRIVING

✸

Rotten Row, the riding path that got its name from a delightfully pointed corruption of 'Route du Roi' (King's Way); the King was William III, who, ironically, died after a fall while riding beside the Thames.

Other terms for routes to and about the gardens include 'chase', mentioned earlier, and 'anfilade' (from the French word *enfilade*, meaning 'line'). This was a coinage by the landscape gardener Stephen Switzer (1682–1745), who worked at Kensington Palace in London and at Blenheim in Oxfordshire: 'The Anfilade or Circuit ought to be six or seven Yards wide at least, and should be carried over the tops of the highest Hills that lie within the Compass of any Nobleman's or Gentleman's Design, though it does not extend to the utmost Extremity of it; and from those Eminencies (whereon, if any where, Building or Clumps of Trees ought to be placed) it is that you are to view the whole Design.' Very much a child of the pictorially obsessed eighteenth century, an anfilade is simply a circuitous drive offering views from high ground. Remaining examples are usually referred to as 'drives'.

THE STATE OF THE ROADS

IF YOU APPROACH a historic garden via a long entrance drive across parkland, it is very unlikely to be the original road. This is not only because scenic drives were the creation of the late eighteenth century and after; it is also because solid, reliable roads are a comparatively recent invention. Until the late eighteenth century the best roads in England were those left behind by the Romans over 1000 years earlier. The technique of laying roads did not seriously advance beyond Roman achievements before the early years of the nineteenth century; and outside the major arterial routes, broken stone and flint roads were the norm right up until the beginning of the twentieth century. During the 1790s, Humphry Repton was urging country house owners to stop using simple grass drives to get to their front doors and to start laying gravel ones, and though a grass drive might seem impractical to us, it was still a common feature at the end of the nineteenth century. We should imagine the effect of entering a great estate by carriage along the typical grass drive: the difference in comfort, in turning from the harsh, jolting high road to the soft turf; the difference in sound, when horses' hoofs and iron-rimmed wheels move from broken stone to grass. The approach to the garden is already one of magical seclusion.

▦ Reading the Entrance & Beyond

Driving across parkland in order to reach an historic garden gives an excellent opportunity to experience just how accomplished the eighteenth- and nineteenth-century landscape improvers were. A good entrance drive has to perform a number of functions alongside the necessary ones of comfort and convenience. The drive has to show off the proprietor's land – its extent, fertility and its 'beauties' or pictorial qualities. An artfully winding drive can make the owner's possessions seem larger, but one that runs near land obviously belonging to someone else will have the opposite effect. It has to ensure that we approach the house from the right perspective, with the right setting – it mustn't, for example, make the house look too small, too squat, or somehow out of place in the landscape. Above all, it has to make our entrance into this demesne a dramatic one: it has to use suspense and anticipation, giving us tantalizing peeps of the house on the way (a characteristic of Brownian landscapes) before revealing the whole in its most imposing aspect.

Finally, before we actually set foot in the garden, it's worth considering just exactly where we find it. The setting and orientation of a house and garden can give us important clues about their age and about what we should expect to encounter once inside them.

SETTING

Although most houses are subject to a lesser degree of change than their gardens, it's nevertheless true that few country houses stand in exactly the same spot on which they were first built. Hatfield House, for example, one of the greatest Jacobean houses in England, does not quite occupy the site of the original house, Hatfield Palace (Queen Elizabeth I's childhood home), which stood about 100 yards (90 m) to the northwest. Similarly, Newby Hall in Yorkshire was built not quite on the site of the original medieval hall, which stood a little way to the south. In both cases the new house was built on slightly higher ground, with better views – not least over the gardens, which would be redesigned and relaid to suit the new setting. By way of contrast, Blickling Hall in Norfolk, though very similar in design to Hatfield, is built precisely on the old site (and foundations) of its medieval predecessor – probably in order to save money. Its setting is rather low in relation to the gardens; generally speaking, over the centuries country houses have moved to higher ground rather than the other way round. If an historic house that

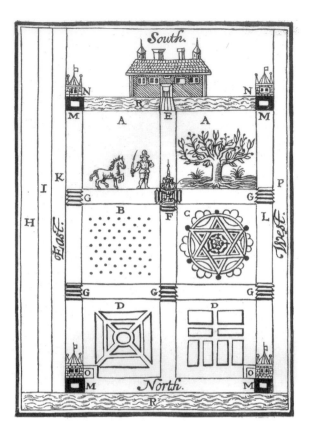

ABOVE: *An early Jacobean plan showing ornamental and productive gardens on the north side of the house.*

you visit does seem to be set rather low in relation to the garden, it may well be because it occupies the same site it always did, and that the gardens themselves occupy a site perhaps unchanged since the Middle Ages.

ORIENTATION

THE OTHER VERY COMMON change to be aware of is in the orientation of the house and garden. Surprisingly few historic houses face the same direction as they did when first built: very often the site of the main entrance has been changed, and that usually means changing the site of the gardens too. This is true of both Hatfield House and Newby Hall. For two centuries after it was built in 1607, Hatfield House was entered from the south, through Hatfield Forest. During the nineteenth century the entrance was reversed so that the house was entered from the north (which was also the side nearest the railway station), and the seventeenth-century gardens below the north front were buried under tarmac. Newby Hall's entrance was changed from the west to the east front in the late eighteenth century, with corresponding changes in the gardens nearby. Hatfield's is the commonest alteration. Moving the entrance away from the south and freeing up that side of the house for private rooms is a typical nineteenth-century improvement, allowing owners to explore the benefits of sunny drawing rooms and libraries. Humphry Repton, who recommended that the private rooms of a house should always face southeast, estimated that he had changed the orientation of the entrance front in 'at least one half of the houses submitted to my opinion'. No entrance from the south means a chance to create new gardens on that side of the house, which is one reason why even the oldest houses may have nineteenth-century gardens on their south side.

TREES & HEDGES

*Forests were the first temples of the Divinity, and it is in the forests
that men have grasped the first idea of architecture.*

FRANÇOIS-RENE DE CHATEAUBRIAND

TREES ARE ALMOST invariably the first things we encounter in an historic garden, with hedges perhaps a close second. As we enter a country estate, the belt of trees we pass through may be the first indication that a change of ownership has taken place in the landscape. Alternatively, there may be denser woodland, with grassy tree-lined rides. The drive or approach that our car passes down may also be lined with trees, regularly or irregularly planted. The parkland around us will be punctuated by small clumps or individual specimen trees that act as eye-catchers. There may be a formal avenue of trees – sometimes of dramatic length – leading us to the house. Within the gardens, straight or flowing lines of trees will divide garden spaces and define walks; and there will be more specimen trees, occasionally grouped into an arboretum, and groves planted to form a wilderness or woodland garden.

Trees have been cultivated in England since neolithic times about 10,000 years ago, and the skills of coppicing and pollarding – to create branches about 3 feet (1 m) in length – have been practised for nearly as long. This is the periodic harvesting of branches from 1 to 4 m in length, for posts, poles, thatching spars, baskets, even arrows. In coppicing the tree is cut down to ground level; in pollarding the harvesting is done at around head height. Both methods

LEFT: *Pleached limes at Rofford Manor, Oxfordshire, their trunks nestling in clipped dwarf box.*

encourage the tree to sprout numerous new branches; both have the effect of slowing down a tree's rate of growth, and extending its life almost indefinitely. It's still possible to find medieval coppiced trees dating back 800 years and more. If in a country estate you see an oak with a very thick trunk but with a multitude of branches diverging at head height or a little higher, this is almost certainly a medieval or tudor pollard that has been allowed to grow in later centuries as the practice became less common.

Since at least the Roman occupation of Britain some 2000 years ago, trees have also been grown for their fruit. The planting of orchards was encouraged by the monasteries (see Chapter Four for more about this), but for now we will simply note that the medieval orchard was as much as place of recreation as of production, where trees were valued for their shade and blossom, and that this aesthetic delight is an abiding one. Both medieval and Tudor gardens used trees to shade and give privacy to walks, but it was arguably in the seventeenth and eighteenth centuries that trees came into their own, and the reasons for planting them multiplied: to create dramatic entrances through long avenues; to offer cover for game as the expertise of gunsmiths developed; to provide a suitably diverse landscape in which to take exercise, whether on horseback, by carriage or on foot; to provide definition and a framework for fine views; and, of course, to stand as beautiful specimens in themselves – a fashion especially boosted by the arrival of exotic American imports.

LEFT: *The late 17th-century ideal of high clipped architectural hedges – in this case, shaped as columns to complement the stone statues and fountain.*

CHAPTER TWO:
TREES &
HEDGES

NATIVE TREES

A 'NATIVE' TREE is one that has not been introduced to a country by human means. In the British Isles that is effectively any tree that has been present since Britain and Ireland became cut off from Europe following the end of the last Ice Age, approximately 8500 years ago. There are relatively few of them:

Alder (*Alnus glutinosa*)

Ash (*Fraxinus excelsior*)

Aspen (*Populus tremula*)

Beech (*Fagus sylvatica*)

Bay willow (*Salix pentandra*)

Bird cherry (*Prunus padus*)

Black poplar (*Populus nigra*)

Box (*Buxus sempervirens*)

Common oak (*Quercus robur*)

Crab apple (*Malus sylvestris*)

Crack willow (*Salix fragilis*)

Downy birch (*Betula pubescens*)

Field maple (*Acer campestre*)

Goat willow (*Salix caprea*)

Hawthorn (*Crataegus monogyna*)

Hazel (*Corylus avellana*)

Holly (*Ilex aquifolium*)

Hornbeam (*Carpinus betula*)

Juniper (*Juniperus communis*)

Large-leaved lime (*Tilia platyphyllos*)

Midland thorn (*Crataegus laevigata*)

Rowan (*Sorbus aucuparia*)

Scots pine (*Pinus sylvestris*)

Sessile oak (*Quercus petraea*)

Silver birch (*Betula pendula*)

Small-leaved lime (*Tilia cordata*)

Strawberry tree (*Arbutus unedo*)

Whitebeam (*Sorbus aria*)

White willow (*Salix alba*)

Wild cherry (*Prunus avium*)

Wild service tree (*Sorbus torminalis*)

Wych elm (*Ulmus glabra*)

Yew (*Taxus baccata*)

Is there under heaven a more glorious and refreshing object of the kind, than an impregnable Hedge…?
JOHN EVELYN

HEDGES

HISTORICALLY, HEDGES (particularly hawthorn) have been used to control the movement of animals – and not just on farms. Julius Caesar observed the Belgian tribesmen called the Nervii laying hedges to stop cavalry charges, which they did very effectively. This quality gives hedges a special value. In Elizabethan times, for example, the crime of hedge-breaking was severely punished. For a landowner, livestock are a capital asset, and the strength of a hedge is as important to the stockman as the strength of the vault is to the bank manager. Of course, hedges keep out people too: Elizabethan orchards were hedged with thorns to keep the ripening fruit safe from scrumpers.

Hedges mark the frontiers of the very largest and smallest gardens: they divide the garden from the wider landscape, and the different parts of the garden from each other. For other plants they provide the best shelter from wind and rough weather: a solid wall will create its own mini-cyclone, but a hedge will let just enough breeze through. For humans they offer shade and privacy – sometimes too much shade if a neighbour has planted the kind of evergreen hybrid never intended to be restricted to suburban heights.

For some, the hedge's greatest garden contribution is architectural, a living green 'sculpture' that can be extended into walls, coaxed into niches, and clipped into hundreds of shapes. In simple, linear or curvilinear form, it can be abundantly decorative in knots, or playful in mazes.

The very oldest hedges are simply barriers; the Old English word *hegg* refers to either hedge or fence. Some of these do in fact survive in the countryside. It is sometimes thought that English country hedges are a creation of the eighteenth century – the age of enclosure. It's true that a great many field hedges were planted in this era, but a country hedge today is just as likely to date from Shakespeare's time or even earlier: more than one hedge has been dated at over 1000 years old. Indeed, hedge remains have been found in the excavations of Roman forts – and it seems likely that the hedges were here before the Romans.

Hedges do, however, owe a debt to the Romans. Fascinated by husbandry, the Romans produced guides to hedge-laying that were in use centuries later. If you want to lay a hedge in a long, straight, Roman line, soak an old rope in a solution with thorn seeds, then stretch the rope straight and bury it in a shallow trench. Simple. The Romans also had a highly developed sense of the ornamental value of hedges, shaping them in the form of letters and animals. That ornamental value was rediscovered in England during the sixteenth and seventeenth centuries, and to a great extent remains with us today (for further detail, see pages 85–8).

Medieval gardeners made great use of hedging plants, including box, yew, juniper, bay and holly, to form arbours and bowers. One of the great contributions of late medieval and Tudor gardens is the creation of the 'knot'. Once thought of as quintessentially Elizabethan, knots are now known to have been laid in the reign of Elizabeth's grandfather, Henry VII (r. 1485–1509), though it's true that they reached their most dazzling elaboration in the late sixteenth century. In the seventeenth and early eighteenth centuries the structural, architectural use of hedges predominated, whether as low lines of box to edge a parterre, or high palissades of hornbeam to give crisp definition to the lines of a grove. That architectural use was modified by English experience of foreign gardens – especially Italian ones – in which a dark, close-cropped hedge might form the perfect frame to a piece of ancient sculpture. Outside the garden a more prosaic but controversial explosion of hedging was taking place across the countryside following the Enclosure Acts of the 1720s and after. It has been estimated that around 200,000 miles (320,000 km) of hedge, most of them

ABOVE: *This woodcut from the 15th-century* Hypnerotomachia Poliphili *is by an unknown Italian master, possibly a sculptor, and shows an elaborate and highly architectural design for an arbour.*

PREVIOUS PAGE: *A box parterre at Broughton
Castle, Oxfordshire, first laid out in the 1880s,
when historical gardening came back into fashion.*

hawthorn, were laid to enclose farmland. Much of this agricultural hedging was grubbed up in the later twentieth century, though farmers today are subsidized to replace rather than remove hedges.

Hedge planting in the nineteenth century was driven by a number of factors. One of these was a rediscovered delight in the old formal garden and its clipped hedges – a fashionable reaction against the informalities of the landscape garden. The restoration of the extraordinary topiary garden at Levens Hall in Cumbria in the early years of the century was an important landmark in this respect. Another factor was the proliferation of new, fast-growing species of conifer, often imported from the Pacific coastlines of Chile, North America and Japan, and with an astonishing range of leaf colours. The gardens at Elvaston mentioned earlier were planted with 11 miles (18 km) of evergreen hedges in every shade of gold, silver, blue and green foliage possible. A third factor was the creation of thousands of small gardens to accompany the terraced houses springing up on the edges of towns and cities throughout Britain, many of which marked their boundaries with hedges – in many cases privet, though beech and holly were also favoured. Finally, when the passion for reviving seventeenth-century formality passed, the Arts and Crafts movement could still give an impulse to the planting of 'traditional' yew and box hedges, which carried its own momentum through to the twentieth century and its rediscovery of the architectural lines of the Italian Renaissance garden. It's ironic that a garden form as old as the hedge finally, perhaps, came into its own in the early years of the twentieth century, with the creation of gardens such as Hidcote and Sissinghurst and their perfectly proportioned divisions of yew and beech.

▦ ALLEYS & *ALLÉES*

AN ALLEY, from the old French word *allée*, is simply a 'walk'. It has been with us since not long after the Normans invaded in the eleventh century, and there are alleys described by Geoffrey Chaucer in *The Canterbury Tales* (*c.* 1387). Inevitably, a number of variations have flourished, of which the most delightful must surely be the pleached alley. To 'pleach' is to bend and interweave branches: eventually adjacent trees graft together, creating a living barrier, either upright or arched, that requires no artificial support. Originally, pleaching was applied primarily to vines in order to form them into hedges (vines were the most popular

How Old Is that Hedge?

THE DATING OF HEDGES is even more uncertain than that of trees. It's not possible to ring-count them, and as hedges are capable of renewing themselves, the very youngest hedge plants may simply be descendants of the most ancient ancestors. Hedges in gardens will quite often have their planting date recorded – the head gardener should know. Hedges outside the garden are a different matter. There is, however, a rule of thumb for the hedge detective, known as Hooper's Rule, after naturalist Dr Max Hooper (b.1934). Here's how it works.

Take any 100-foot (30-m) stretch of hedge. Count the number of different species of trees and shrubs in it. That number will be roughly equivalent to the age of the hedge in centuries, so six species would equal 600 years. Of course, this is only an approximate guide. If your hedge has more than five species in it, and you want to be sure that it belongs to the time of Elizabeth I, not Elizabeth II, have a look at the route it takes across country. Medieval and Tudor hedges follow ancient field boundaries, which are generally very irregular. A long, straight hedge is unlikely to be an ancient one.

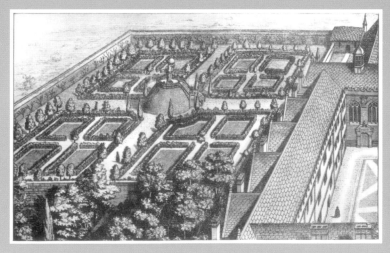

RIGHT: *Formal hedge planting provided meditative walkways for the dons of Wadham College, Oxford, in the 17th century.*

RIGHT: *A pleached alley can provide a dramatic architectural feature in a garden. This example is from Oak Spring in Virginia.*

shade-giving plant in the medieval garden). By Elizabethan times the practice had extended to orchard trees, such as apple and pear. The pleaching provided both shade and privacy, which is why in Shakespeare's *Much Ado About Nothing* (1600) the 'thick-pleached alley' in Antonio's orchard is the place where everyone goes to make declarations of love. As the pleasure garden expanded, so did pleaching: in the early eighteenth century you might particularly find it in any extended wooded area where a green wall was required. Hornbeam was the favoured pleaching tree, followed by lime and elm: some ancient pleached lime alleys endure to this day. But the great majority of pleached trees that you see in today's gardens are likely to be re-creations of the nineteenth or twentieth century.

The second important type of alley is the bowling alley. Different kinds of bowls have been played in England since the thirteenth century, and this type of alley represents one of the most common, formal uses of grass in the garden. It's one that we will consider in detail in the next chapter.

The third type of alley is also known as an *allée*. This, as its name suggests, is a development of French gardening. An *allée* is a straight, formal path, sometimes tree-lined, that gives structure to the garden. *Allées* have been a feature of French royal gardens since at least 1614, when a gardener was contracted to take care of the *allées* and *palissades* (hedges clipped to imitate walls) in the Tuileries in Paris. It was this kind of alley that later developed into the avenue. These French-inspired alleys invaded England at the time of the Restoration (1660), and provided the formal skeleton for the geometric layouts favoured by London and Wise at the Brompton Park Nursery (and their numerous imitators). There were formal alleys in English gardens before the Restoration – Francis Bacon describes them lovingly in his *Essays* (1597–1625) – but they didn't have quite the domineering quality of their French cousins. When the pendulum swung towards natural, informal landscape gardens in the following century, *allées* became symptomatic of all that was unimaginative and constrictive in the old French designs. Alexander Pope famously satirized them in his *Epistle to Lord Burlington* (1731):

> *No pleasing intricacies intervene,*
> *No artful wildness to perplex the scene;*
> *Grove nods at grove, each alley has a brother,*
> *And half the platform just reflects the other.*

Any garden that still retains something of the formal layout of the seventeenth century will provide good examples of *allées*. They needn't be tree-lined (or hedge-lined) – they might simply be formal paths betweens beds of flowers on a parterre – but they will be formal.

ARBORETA

AN ARBORETUM (from the Latin *arbor*, meaning tree) is a botanical garden for trees. The word seems to have been first defined in English by the gardening writer J.C. Loudon in 1838, and for that reason the arboretum that he helped found at Derby in 1840 is sometimes claimed as the world's first. A much older claim is advanced by Trsteno Arboretum in Croatia, which celebrated its 500th anniversary in 1994, though there's no evidence that it was actually described as an arboretum in the fifteenth century. In fact, the birth of the arboretum belongs

LEFT: *Lime has long been one of the most favoured trees for pleaching, as in this example from The Laskett, Herefordshire.*

CHAPTER TWO:
TREES &
HEDGES
✺

not to Europe at all, but to America, and in particular to the Quaker communities of the eastern seaboard. The Quaker emphasis on God's living presence in the world fostered a tradition of nature lovers and gardeners. The state of Pennsylvania, founded by the Quaker William Penn in 1682, was home to some of the finest eighteenth-century botanists, notably the Bartram family of Kingsessing, who sent many newly discovered American plants to England. It was John Bartram who published the first great plant book of America, *Arboretum Americanum, the American Grove, or an Alphabetical Catalogue of Forest Trees Native of the American United States* (1775), beating Loudon by over half a century. Bartram's cousin Humphry Marshall planted an arboretum across the state in the same decade, while another Quaker family, the Peirces, laid out their own version in the 1780s.

One of the delights for American botanists in the eighteenth century was the sheer number and variety of as yet uncatalogued trees. John Bartram discovered dozens of new specimens, for which he found a ready market in England. English estates such as Fonthill (Wiltshire) began laying out 'American gardens' to receive the new imports; it is these that are the precursors of the English arboreta of the nineteenth century. The chief difference in the model espoused by Loudon was that he moved in the Victorian tradition of public works: motives such as health, exercise and education were just as important as the unalloyed enjoyment of the natural world.

A surprising number of private gardens have arboreta attached to them, many created in the past hundred years. For a comprehensive display of tree species you would expect a certain amount of space to be required. It's true that the historic arboretum at Westonbirt in Gloucestershire runs to 600 acres (240 hectares); but Westonbirt's slightly younger cousin at Derby occupies only 162 acres (65 hectares) – a mere paddock for some country house gardens.

An arboretum displaying only evergreen trees is called a 'pinetum': there is a good example at Bedgebury in Kent.

✸ AVENUES

WE TEND TO THINK of any straight, regularly planted line of trees as an avenue. Strictly speaking, the avenue is the road or walkway besides which the trees are planted. Very strictly speaking, the word should apply only to the road leading up to the entrance of the house – the road by which we come in: 'avenue' being a child of the French *advenir*, to come.

The word 'avenue' was first defined in English by John Evelyn (1620–1706) in his book *Sylva, or a Discourse of Forest-Trees and the Propagation of Timber*: 'That this may yet be no prejudice to the meaner capacities let them read for *avenue*, the principal walk to the front of the house, or seat.' (Evelyn built a great reputation for himself on the back of knowledge invariably stolen from others, and never passed up an opportunity to make 'the meaner capacities' feel really ignorant.) *Sylva*, and its publication date – 1664 – are often cited as the start of a great renaissance in tree planting, avenue laying and all kinds of arboreal enterprise. Certainly the great age of avenue planting dates from the late seventeenth century, and Evelyn played his part in promoting that planting – as he did in promoting anything for which he might claim some credit. But the first avenues in England are a little older than this – and it wasn't John Evelyn who created them.

Evelyn seems to have coined the word 'avenue' at least ten years earlier, using it in his journal descriptions of houses and gardens that he visited. Almost certainly he picked it up in France, to which he paid several extended visits during the years of the English Civil Wars (1642–51) and the Commonwealth (1649–53). In France the avenue was a new concept too. The French in the early eighteenth century had made great use of straight walks lined with trees, but these were called *allées*, not avenues. Their function was to give structure to the garden, not to dramatize the entrance. The man who popularized 'advenues' was the royal gardener André Mollet (see page 36). Having worked in courts throughout Europe (including the English one), Mollet in 1651 decreed that the ideal royal palace should be approached by 'une grande advenuë' with a double or triple row of elms or limes aligned perpendicularly with the entrance. John Evelyn was in France (and visiting gardens) when Mollet's book was published, so it seems likely that he found the idea there.

But Mollet had been working in England for Charles I and Henrietta Maria before the Civil War began and almost certainly planted avenues at that time. Mollet created the gardens for Queen Henrietta Maria's house at Wimbledon in 1642, which included an avenue of limes (later felled by the Parliamentarians when they ransacked the house). Mollet apparently also worked at St James's Palace in the 1620s, though what he was up to we do not know. We mentioned earlier, however, John Evelyn's diary and its record of houses and gardens Evelyn had visited in the 1650s. Intriguingly, some of these are described by Evelyn as possessing avenues, which must have been planted in the 1620s, or even earlier. One of those gardens was that of Newhall, near Chelmsford in Essex, which had been owned by George Villiers, Duke of Buckingham, before

the Civil War, and which had a 'Sweete & faire avenue planted with stately Lime-trees in 4 rowes for neere a mile in length'. Villiers' gardener had been the redoubtable John Tradescant (1570–1638), and this avenue was probably Jacobean in origin. Another Jacobean avenue stood at Audley End in Essex, where the gardens had been laid out to entertain King James himself between 1608 and 1614. Even more fascinating is 'the avenue planted with rows of faire Elmes' spotted by Evelyn at the old royal palace of Nonsuch (near Ewell in Surrey) – though many of the trees had again been 'fell'd by those destructive & avaritious Rebells in the late Warr'. No major work is recorded at Nonsuch after 1591, so these trees were probably planted earlier and may be the first major avenue in England. The date itself ties in with another ancient avenue that we know to have been planted at Hengrave, Suffolk, in the 1580s. It looks as though the English avenue may in fact be an Elizabethan creation, and not one of the seventeenth century after all.

How Old
Is that Tree?

VERY FEW TREES reach their natural lifespan. This is partly because the great majority of trees inhabit a managed landscape and we simply don't leave them alone for long enough. An oak planted at the beginning of the eighteenth century might, with luck, live to the twenty-eighth century, but it would have been ripe for felling in the middle of the nineteenth century, when prices for timber were good and an estate owner might pay off a mortgage by cutting down and selling mature trees. Acre for acre, Victorian landowners made more money from timber than from arable crops. Most country estates, then, have very few trees over 200 years old: they are an asset that needs to be used.

Longevity also depends on how and where the oak was grown, how fast it grew and, most importantly, how it was managed. Like any tall structure, a tree needs good foundations if it is to stand for long. An oak that is self-seeded will probably develop a better root structure than one that has been transplanted to a park or garden. On the other hand, an oak that is planted in a park will have much more light and space than one that grows as a seedling in a wood. Ironically, this is likely to shorten its life: its branches will grow much faster, and it is ultimately more likely to become top-heavy and run the risk of being blown down in a storm. By the same token, the ancient forms of managing trees help extend their lives: coppicing slows down the rate of growth and means that the root system will never be strained by the tree's 'superstructure' (this also means that the biggest trees are not necessarily the oldest). On balance – and laying aside factors such as disease and pests – the very oldest trees are likely to be those whose growth has been stunted in some way, whether by medieval (or later) management, or by natural means such as drought.

Dating a tree accurately is impossible to do without either cutting it down and counting the rings, or drilling a core sample, which although not deadly, will be very stressful for the tree. The conventional rule of thumb is this: measure the girth (circumference) of the tree at breast-height (roughly 5 feet or 150 cm). If the tree is standing alone in a park, calculate one year of age for every 1 inch (2.5 cm) of girth. If the tree is in a wood and hemmed in by other trees, calculate one year of age for every 2 inches (5 cm) of girth.

ABOVE: *A veteran tree will always show its age. Branches may be lost or die back, but the heartwood will remain strong for centuries. This veteran is at Old Sleningford, Yorkshire.*

The great age of avenue creation coincided with the domination of English landscape by the royal gardeners George London (?–1714) and Henry Wise (?–1738). London founded the Brompton Park Nursery in 1681, and Wise went into partnership with him a few years later. The nursery covered an area of almost 100 acres (40 hectares) – now occupied by the Victorian & Albert Museum – and it supplied trees and plants on a prodigious scale: quite literally thousands each month. London and Wise planted avenues at Longleat in Wiltshire, Chatsworth and Melbourne in Derbyshire, Petworth in Sussex, Castle Howard in Yorkshire,

Blenheim in Oxfordshire and Hampton Court in Surrey, among many others. The bill for Longleat alone ran to £30,000 (the equivalent of £4 million today), which helps to explain why Henry Wise left a fortune of £100,000 (over £10 million at present rates) on his death.

London and Wise's preferred avenue trees were elm and lime. They disliked oak (it grows too slowly) and beech (it doesn't like being transplanted) – and indeed elm and lime, with their graceful, upright habits, were the avenue trees of choice right up to Victorian times. The deaths of London, Wise and their pupil Charles Bridgeman (see page 36) mark the end of the great fashion for avenue planting. However, the arrival of new trees in the mid-nineteenth century, especially exotic evergreens from across the Atlantic, gave the avenue a new lease of life. Quite a number of gardens possess avenues of giant redwoods (first introduced to England in 1853) that dwarf anything conceived at Brompton Park, while Bicton in Devon has a 550-yard (500-m) avenue of monkey puzzles, planted in 1843. The supreme example of this kind of excess was (and is) Elvaston in Derbyshire, where evergreen avenues were planted in quadruple and even quintuple lines for about half a mile (1 km) in front of the house.

If you see an evergreen avenue, it almost certainly dates from the nineteenth century and after. If, however, the avenue is deciduous and long, the chances are that it dates from the early eighteenth century. The trees themselves are less likely to be original. If they were elm, they would have been killed by Dutch elm disease in the 1970s. Any other avenue species planted in the early eighteenth century would be reaching the end of its natural life by the close of the twentieth century. If there are stretches of younger trees interspersed, these may have been planted to replace trees felled by the Great Storm of 1987. Avenues always present garden restorers with a problem: if you replace individual trees as they sicken, the young trees create awkward gaps in the line of the avenue; if you replace the whole avenue in one go, you preserve a consistent line, but you have to wait sixty years for it to reach the right height.

GROVES

A GROVE IS DEFINED quite simply as 'a small wood'. In historic gardens it is, so to speak, more of a genus than a species – spelt with a small 'g'. As a named place, you are just as likely to find 'The Grove' in a postal address as in a garden. The definition tells us what a grove is, but it hardly begins to tells us what it represents.

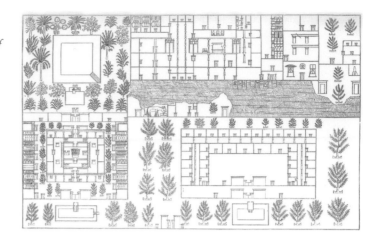

In classical Greek and Roman culture a grove was a sacred, magical space. There was a famous grove of oaks at Dodona, which could foretell the future, and another of olives at Delphi, the seat of the Oracle. The Roman poet Ovid (43 BC–AD 17) made the grove an integral part of his iconic *locus amoenus* (lovely place) – a group of trees, a spring or brook, a grassy meadow – where magic might take place. These ideas conditioned European notions of the perfect garden for centuries. Their persistence was partly due to the admiration of later ages for classical learning. But there must also be a possibility that they reflect a genuine and abiding experience: the entry into a small, self-enclosed group of trees does give rise to a feeling of moving from one type of space into one more special and rarefied, an atmosphere that is not quite our own. The Latin word for 'grove', *nemus*, sometimes refers not just to the trees, but more specifically to the space within them: groves are meant to be walked into, not around.

The grove as a garden feature is a characteristic of the seventeenth century. For gardeners of the Restoration it was a small group of trees planted within a pleasure garden, a miniature evocation of idealized woodland. John Evelyn gave his readers instructions for planting 'a grove for pleasure'. The royal gardeners London and Wise were more prescriptive, not to say pedantic:

> *A Grove…is a Plot of Ground, more or less, as you think fit, enclos'd in Palisades of Horn-beam, the Middle of it fill'd with tall Trees, as Elms or the like, the Tops of which make the Tuft or Plume.*
>
> *At the Foot of the Elms, which should grow along the Palisades at equal Distances, other Wild Trees should be planted, and the Tuft that will by this means be form'd in the Inside, will resemble that of a Copse.*

There were groves in royal gardens: one of oaks in Hyde Park was uprooted in 1730 to make way for the Serpentine lake.

RIGHT AND BELOW RIGHT: *Designs for knots are a
common feature of early gardening books. The
examples on this page are from the* Maison Rustique
of 1600, and from William Lawson's The Country
House-wife's Garden *of 1618.*

The word 'grove' itself is one of provoking mystery. Most words in English, including those
used in the garden, have their ancestors or cousins in the old Germanic languages, in Latin or
Greek, or occasionally in Celtic. 'Grove', however, just appears, fully formed; there is no word
like it in any other tongue. It is used in Old English to describe a small wood; whether there
are any sacred or symbolic overtones is less certain. The Celtic (and, some would say, Druidic)
version was *llannerch*, which became, intriguingly, the word *llann*, meaning 'church'.

MAZES

THESE STRUCTURES OF artful perplexity clearly exercise a powerful hold upon the
imagination. In the British landscape their earliest form is the turf maze or labyrinth, which is,
as its name suggests, simply a maze cut in turf. There may once have been hundreds of these in
England – they are associated with communal celebrations and dances, rather like may-poles.
Now there are some half a dozen remaining. These turf mazes were probably cut in medieval
times; similar examples can be found in mosaic form in the floors of medieval cathedrals such
as Chartres, where their elaborate turns can symbolise the journey of the errant soul towards
salvation. Having said that, the proximity of some turf mazes to ancient monuments such as
burial mounds might suggest an even earlier origin. Writing in the first century AD, Pliny the
Elder describes children playing in something like a turf maze in the Field of Mars just outside
the walls of Rome: did the first maze designs arrive in Britain courtesy of the Romans?

Hedge mazes in English gardens date from the sixteenth century. Their designs were
probably influenced by mazes in French and Italian gardens. Cut at first with low plants, such
as thyme and hyssop, by the early years of the seventeenth century hornbeam was becoming a
favourite plant, and mazes were reaching their familiar height of 6 feet (2 m). The great maze
at Hampton Court was first planted in hornbeam in 1690 (it has since been replanted in yew),
though it is a minnow compared to its vast predecessor at Versailles.

Like many once-common formal features of the sixteenth and seventeenth centuries, mazes
fell out of favour during the eighteenth century, but were revived by the Victorians. A number
of country house mazes, including those at Hatfield House in Hertfordshire and Glendurgan
in Cornwall, were first planted (or replanted) in the 1840s and after. Victorian maze creators
favoured evergreens such as yew over deciduous hornbeam: the classic idea of the maze cut in

dark green monumental yew is very much a nineteenth-century creation. In recent years the popularity of mazes has been boosted by the cutting of crop mazes. Originally an American idea, crop mazes are cut in tall, quick-growing crops such as (inevitably) maize, and provide a summer's entertainment before being cut down at harvest.

For the technically minded, mazes can be either unicursal (having one route) or multicursal (having many routes). The devious multicursal varieties are likely to be of later invention.

▨ KNOTS & KNOT GARDENS

KNOTS AND KNOT GARDENS are one of the distinctively English contributions to the garden world. Indeed, there is something uncompromisingly Anglo-Saxon about the word 'knot' – as hard and unnegotiable as a tightly tied rope itself. The irony, of course, is that the pattern the word has come to describe can be one of infinite delicacy and variation. The idea of the ornamental knot first came to life in the Middle Ages – not at first in gardens, but in heraldry and in stone carving. Sir Gawain, one of the knights of the Round Table, is described in a medieval poem as carrying a shield embossed with a pentangle, the lines of which cross and uncross without beginning or end – 'which in English is called "the endless knot"'. Medieval monasteries are also described as having pillars 'carved with curious knots'. It was these designs, part heraldic, part architectural, that crossed into the garden.

Perhaps unsurprisingly, the first knot garden known to us was a royal one – at Richmond in Surrey. Here, in Henry VII's new palace, completed in 1501, there were 'most fair and pleasant gardens, with royal knots alleyed and herbed; many marvellous beasts, as lions, dragons, and such other of divers kind, properly fashioned and carved in the ground, right well sanded, and compassed with lead; with many vines, seeds and strange fruit, rightly beset'. We have no pictorial record of these knots, but from the description it seems clear that the heraldic designs dominated, and it was probably these that spread to the gardens of the nobility: the Duke of Buckingham, whose gardener was paid three shillings and fourpence in 1502 'for diligence in making knottes in the Duke's garden', and the Duke of Northumberland, whose gardener was

LEFT: *Simple knots laid out in box in the gardens at Badminton, Gloucestershire.*
RIGHT: *Another design from* Maison Rustique, *originally written by Charles Estienne (1505–64), printer to the French King Francis II.*

CHAPTER TWO:
TREES &
HEDGES
✶

paid for 'clypping of knottes' in the same year. With such distinguished supporters, the fashion seems to have spread quickly: in a few years the term 'knot garden' was common enough to enter schoolbooks. William Harmon, headmaster of Eton College, taught his pupils in 1516 that 'The knot-garden serveth for pleasure: the potte garden for profitte' – an important distinction.

By the end of the sixteenth century, knots could be found in every middle-class garden. They were planted in thyme, hyssop, thrift (armeria), germander (teucrium), savory, marjoram and box. 'Open knots' left interior planting space to frame the commonest flowers to dramatic effect; the more tightly woven forms left (and required) no space for further planting. Knots were small, beautiful and capable of being infinitely personalized; like a convenient pet, they required enough attention to sustain the gardener's interest, but not enough to burden it. Small wonder they became so popular. William Lawson provides plans for nine different types of knot, but makes clear that this is very much the tip of the iceberg: 'The number of formes, Mazes and Knots is so great, and men are so diversly delighted that I leave every House-wife to her self, especially seeing to set downe many, had been but to fill much paper' (note that pleasure gardens were a woman's province, and remained such for centuries). Francis Bacon, on the other hand, who was not only Lord Chancellor but the man responsible for one of central London's most popular gardens at Gray's Inn, was notoriously dismissive: 'you may see as good sights many times in tarts'. The sneers of the mighty at a particular garden feature can tell us much about its popularity, just as their hasty adoption of it a century earlier advertises its novelty.

At the time that Bacon was writing, Charles I's queen, Henrietta Maria, was inviting André Mollet over from Paris to design her garden in the new French fashion. Mollet created not knots, but parterres (see pages 129–30). In fact, his father, Jacques, was said to have invented them for the French king Henri IV. It sounds like the death knell of a fashion being rung: 125 years from one royal garden at Richmond to another at Wimbledon. Of course, the reality was not so straightforward. Although the swirls of a seventeenth-century, French-inspired parterre may seem to us a world away from the complex interweavings of an Elizabethan knot, the difference at the time may not have seemed so great. What we think of as parterres (including those at Wimbledon) were being called 'knots' right up to the end of the seventeenth century: no doubt the new French forms simply appeared to be variations on the old English ones. Ironically, the term 'parterre' vanquished the term 'knot' only a few years before all such elaboration was condemned to the graveyard of fashion by the new openness of the landscape garden.

There are no original knot gardens in Britain. Although a box hedge can live in theory for 300 years, in practice you need a gardener to clip it for every one of those years. Knots effectively vanished from our gardens until the twentieth century. There were a few Victorian attempts at re-creating them, but it was in the gardens of another royal palace that the art of the knot was finally resurrected. A young barrister, Ernest Law, who was lucky enough to live in an apartment at Hampton Court, developed an obsession with Tudor history. He persuaded the palace authorities to let him plant a knot garden there in 1924, and later planted another in Stratford, at Shakespeare's birthplace. Neither was absolutely authentic, but they were enough to revive interest in these ancient, intertwined art forms. Today there are numerous re-created knot gardens, including a fine one at the Museum of Garden History in London.

QUINCUNXES

IN THE PLANTING ARRANGEMENT called a quincunx five trees are planted so that four occupy the corners of a square or (strictly speaking) a diamond, and one sits in the centre – in the same style as the number five is marked on dice. Two trees of one side then begin the next quincunx, and so on. The term, which comes from the Latin, actually means 'five-twelfths'. The Roman coin known as the *as* weighed a standard 12 ounces (56 g), and five-twelfths of an *as* was written in the form of five dots – just as seen on dice. Later the term came to be used to describe a staggered formation adopted by Roman legionaries in battle. It was this military usage that was taken up by French gardeners in the seventeenth century, with their love of regimented planting lines, and that in turn migrated to England. There was, indeed, a brief moment at the turn of the eighteenth century when great gardens across Europe seemed to be planted as battlefields – Blenheim (perhaps unsurprisingly, as it was named after a battle) was a good example before its replanting by Capability Brown. Orchards were planted in quincuncial form long before the word for the pattern came into use, and it is in orchards that you are most likely to see a quincunx today.

HEDGE PLANTS

DIFFERENT SPECIES OF hedge plant have had their champions, and we review some of those commonly found in historic and modern gardens in the pages following.

BEECH

BEECH IS A NATIVE British tree, but of all the popular hedge plants it is one of the youngest. There are beech hedges at Levens that may have been first planted in the 1680s, and a prodigious specimen planted in 1746 at Meikleour in Aberdeenshire, possibly the largest hedge in the country. There's a tradition that the latter was to be kept uncut in memory of those who died in the battle of Culloden (1746). But the planting of beech trees only really took off in the late eighteenth and nineteenth centuries, and the beech hedge is typical of the Victorian garden. Gardeners like beech hedges because the dead leaves do not fall and rot, but remain a crisp cover on the plant. It's a useful characteristic – beech leaves were once favoured as a stuffing for mattresses, being longer lasting and less liable to rot than straw.

Box

ALTHOUGH WE ASSOCIATE box with the clipped hedges of French and Italian gardens, it is in fact a native British plant. It has been used for hedging and topiary across Europe since Roman times. It is possible that the original sense of the word 'box' itself is 'something made from the wood of the box tree (latin *buxus*)', which was the preferred wood for small containers. Left to its own devices, the box tree will in fact grow quite large – otherwise Maria's suggestion of a hiding-place in *Twelfth Night* – 'get ye all three into the box tree' – would hardly be very practical. Dwarf box is listed in Elizabethan herbals, though in the seventeenth century this

RIGHT: *A recreated Tudor knot garden, laid out in the gardens at Dalemain, Cumbria.*

came to be known as French or Dutch box, no doubt under the influence of formal gardens on the Continent. Both forms were immensely popular in the sixteenth and seventeenth centuries, but there have always been gardeners and garden owners who cannot abide the smell. Queen Anne was a notorious example, uprooting all the box parterres planted by her predecessors William and Mary at Hampton Court and Kensington Palace.

CODLING

A CODLING HEDGE is a curious thing. A codling (sometimes quodling, quadling or querdling – the variations are numerous) is a type of cooking apple, rather sour. In fact, the fruit's sourness resulted in any unripe apple being called a codling. In the sixteenth and seventeenth centuries it was customary to make hedges from fruiting plants, such as vines and apple, pear and plum trees. The apple was perhaps the most popular, possibly because its fragrant blossom gives it a double attraction. So an apple hedge – whether planted with codling apples or not – is sometimes called a codling hedge. At one time they were so fashionable that they became the subject of satire: the eighteenth-century comic writer Richard Graves wrote of the cheesemonger thinking how grand he was 'when smoking his pipe under his codling hedge on his gravel walk made of coal ashes'.

ELM

WHILE ELM IS ONE of the great hedge trees, it is something of a rarity today because we have the misfortune to live at a time of its greatest devastation. Dutch elm disease is caused by an apparently ancient fungus, which in the late 1960s mutated into a virulent form responsible over the next twenty years for the near-extinction of large elms.

LEFT: *A geometrical garden at Ham House, London, based on late-17th-century evidence and restored by the National Trust in the 1970s.*

CHAPTER TWO:
TREES &
HEDGES

As the elm reproduces through suckers rather than seeds, it is capable of taking over an entire hedge once it has established itself. In the seventeenth century elms were so common that John Evelyn's advice to a reader who wanted an elm was to go out and take a spare one from the nearest hedge. Elms were used extensively as ornamental hedges during the late seventeenth and eighteenth centuries. Evelyn described it as 'a Tree of Confort, Sociable, and so affecting to grow in Company…they may be kept plashed, and thickned to the highest twig; affording both a magnificent, and august Defence against the Winds and Sun'. In historic gardens today (Blenheim, for example) they have been replaced by hornbeam or lime.

HAWTHORN

TRADITIONALLY KNOWN AS 'quickset', hawthorn is the king of hedge plants. It is stockproof, quick-growing (hence the old name), and has no objection to being cut and bent into shape. Small wonder, then, that it has been used by everyone from the Ancient Britons onwards. It was laid by the thousand on medieval estates, and in medieval gardens too, where it might be intertwined with roses or honeysuckle.

The Elizabethans found it indispensable: as William Lawson, one of our earliest gardening authorities, noted in 1616, 'neither wood, stone, earth, nor water, can make so strong a fence'. Even today its white blossom brightens spring roadsides throughout Britain. It also, incidentally, has immense ecological value, hosting more wildlife than just about any other British hedge plant.

HOLLY

ANOTHER NATIVE British plant, the holly was known to the Anglo-Saxons, who called it *holen*. Like other native evergreens, the holly is the subject of a rich folklore, including the tradition that the berries had to pass through the bowels of a bird before they would set seed. But the empirical gardeners of the seventeenth century proved otherwise. It was they who really discovered the delights of the holly hedge, though the plant was present in medieval gardens, and had been used as hedging since Tudor times. Once again, the irrepressible John Evelyn took the credit: 'Is there under heaven a more glorious and refreshing object of the kind, than an impregnable Hedge of one hundred and sixty foot in length, seven foot high, and five in diameter, which I can shew in my poor Gardens at any time of the year, glitt'ring with its arm'd and vernish'd leaves? The taller Standards at orderly distances blushing with their natural Corall: it mocks at the rudest assaults of the Weather, Beasts, or Hedge-breaker.'

It is, added Evelyn 'of all our trees the most insensible and stout'. The diarist Samuel Pepys (1633–1703) saw Evelyn's hedges and had to agree – 'the finest things I ever saw in my life' –

though it must have been difficult to disagree with Evelyn in full flow.

In Victorian gardens holly enjoyed a renaissance, thanks in part to the availability of new cultivars, often with beautifully coloured foliage. Many a large golden holly in today's gardens is a relict of the new enthusiasm for the plant in the mid-nineteenth century.

HORNBEAM

HORNBEAM IS AN ancient native tree, harvested to use as fuel as long ago as the Bronze Age. As a hedge plant, its career is more recent, but notably successful. Alongside elm, it was historically the most popular deciduous hedge tree – more popular even than elm where a clipped line was required. John Evelyn explains why: 'it makes the noblest and the stateliest Hedges for long Walks in Gardens, or Parks, of any Tree whatsoever whose leaves are deciduous, and forsake their branches in Winter; because it grows tall, and so sturdy as not to be wronged by the Winds'. Hornbeam was perfect for the French fashion, imported to England in the seventeenth century, for high clipped hedges or palisades, and was much favoured in this respect by the industrious London and Wise. A hornbeam palisade can reach 20 feet (6 m) in height. To learn just how much wordy ecstasy a good hornbeam hedge could provoke in the seventeenth century, it is worth returning to Evelyn:

That admirable Espalier-hedge in the long middle walk of Luxembourg Garden at Paris (than which there is nothing more graceful) is planted of this Tree; and so is that Cradle or Close-walk, with that perplext Canopie, which covers the seat in his Majesties Garden at Hampton-Court. These Hedges are tonsile [able to be clipped]; but where they are maintain'd to fifteen or twenty foot height (which is very frequent in the places before mention'd) they are to be cut, and kept in order with a Sythe of four foot long, and very little falcated [bent like a sickle]; this is fix'd on a long sneed or streight handle, and does wonderfully expedite the trimming of these and the like Hedges.

LAUREL

LAUREL HEDGES ARE not laurel at all – not, that is, the laurel with which the Romans crowned the victors of races. That was *Laurus nobilis*, which we know as bay. In its natural environment the bay will grow to 60 feet (18 m); in England it is usually a delicate standard confined to terracotta pots. The laurel's classical associations meant that it was already widely known in England – during the Middle Ages it was called the 'lorrer'. Thus, the arrival in 1576 of a plant that looked like laurel and could be grown in our climate was a cause for some excitement, which was barely diminished by the fact that it was a cherry, not a laurel. The common laurel, *Prunus laurocenasus*, quickly gained popularity. In 1597 the plantsman John Gerard observed that it was 'well respected for the beauty of the leaves and their lasting or continuall greenenesse'. Since the seventeenth century it has been widely used in hedges – indeed, it was probably overplanted by the Victorians, as was its cousin the Portugal laurel (*Prunus lusitinica*), also a cherry, first introduced in 1648.

LEYLANDII

AN ACCIDENTAL HYBRID, the Leylandii is the hedge tree that was never meant to be. In 1888 a Nootka cypress from Alaska and a Monterey cypress from California were growing side by side in a garden near Powys. One fertilized the other and the result was a new tree, named after the garden owner's brother-in-law, C.J. Leyland. It is the fastest-growing conifer in Britain, distinctly a forest tree (rather a good-looking one) and not in the least suitable for hedges – unless you want one 30 feet (10 m) or more high. But its speed of growth means gardeners get a quick hedge, and its ease of cultivation means nursery owners get a quick profit, so they continue to be planted in the wrong situations, and shaded neighbours continue to fume.

PRIVET

FIRST PLANTED BY Elizabethan gardeners, privet hedges enjoyed rapid popularity. In 1629 the gardener John Parkinson noted that 'the use of this plant is so much, and so frequent throughout all this land, although for no reason but to make hedges or arbours in gardens'. The Victorians planted them in their thousands, in town gardens that no longer required the unforgiving thorns of quickset to keep livestock in or out. Privet excels as a garden hedge. It will stand any amount of cutting – you can chop it right down and it will spring back up again – it keeps out the weather and prying eyes and has creamy-white, sweet-smelling flowers in summer.

YEW

The yew is another species native to Britain, but, unlike other native trees, it has been used by the inhabitants of these islands since the middle of the last ice age. One of the oldest wooden implements in the world is a yew spear-tip found at Clacton-on-Sea in Essex, which has been dated at around 50,000 years old. The oldest trees in Britain are probably also yews – indeed, 'yew' itself is our oldest tree name, deriving from the Celtic word *ew*. Because of its prehistoric associations, and because we are told that yew grows very slowly, we tend to think of yew hedges as having a particular antiquity. In fact, yew is not notably slow-growing: a hedge of it will grow 6 feet (2 m) in ten years, which for historic gardens is the blink of an eye. There are some ancient yew hedges in English gardens, but most are of much more recent date.

The yew was known to medieval and Elizabethan gardeners, though not especially favoured by them as a garden plant. At that time it was the chief source of wood for the English longbow: all the 200 or so bows recovered from Henry VIII's ship the Mary Rose were made of yew, which indicates coppicing on a near-industrial scale. Towards the close of the seventeenth century, John Evelyn sounded a note of alarm: 'Since the use of Bows is laid aside amongst us, the propagation of the Eugh-tree is likewise quite forborn'. In fact, there are some magnificent yew hedges dating from precisely this period at Blickling Hall in Norfolk, and others at Crathes Castle in Aberdeenshire planted in 1702. But the great majority were created in the nineteenth and early twentieth centuries: examples include those at Biddulph Grange in Staffordshire, Hidcote in Gloucestershire and Great Dixter in Sussex.

LEFT: *Topiary yews in the garden at Plas Brondanw, Gwynedd, Wales. One of the myths about yew is that it is very slow-growing. These specimens were probably planted in the early 20th century.*

TOPIARY

TOPIARY WAS INVENTED by the Romans. The earliest description we have of plants cut as topiary comes from Pliny the Elder, who died when Mount Vesuvius erupted in AD74. He describes 'tableaux of *opus topiarium*: hunt scenes, fleets of ships and all sorts of images'. Evidently some skill was involved here, and Pliny's account catapulted the word 'topiary' into the English language. On closer inspection, however, it's clear that Pliny was talking about rather more than just hedge-clipping, and that we have been misusing the word all along. Roman topiary was created by the *topiarius*, whom Pliny noted was responsible for

ABOVE: *Massive topiary pieces in the Cottage Garden at Haddon Hall, Derbyshire. The boar's head and peacock represent the Vernon and Manners families, whose heirs own the hall.*

RIGHT: *Levens is one of the most important and
beautiful topiary gardens in Britain: first laid out in
the late 17th century – though most of the hedging
and topiary work dates from the early 19th century,
when the gardens were restored.*

'woods, groves, hills, fish-ponds, canals, streams, shores'. In fact, 'topiary' refers to all kinds
of landscaping. The word comes from the Greek *topos*, which means 'place', so the *topiarius*
was a place-maker, if you like – a Roman version of the landscape gardener. Be that as it may,
it was the clipping of trees and bushes into sculptural forms that the British came to know
as topiary.

When Renaissance Florence revived classical learning in the fifteenth century, the art of the
topiarius was not excepted. The Villa Rucellai possessed spectacular examples: 'spheres,
porticoes, temples, vases, urns, apes, donkeys, oxen, a bear, giants, men and women, warriors,
a witch, philosophers, popes and cardinals'. It was probably Henry VIII, with his paranoid
determination not to be outdone by the Continent, who introduced topiary to England. *Opere
topiario* (works of topiary) were recorded at Hampton Court in the 1530s, and it may have
been these or their descendants that were seen by the German tourist Thomas Platter in 1599:
'There were all manner of shapes, men and women, centaurs, sirens, serving maids with
baskets, French lilies and delicate crenellations…trimmed and arranged picture-wise that
their equal would be difficult to find.' By the early seventeenth century the practice of topiary
had become widespread. 'Your Gardiner,' William Lawson advised his readers, 'can frame
your lesser wood to the shape of men armed in the field, ready to give battell: or swift-running
Grey Hounds to chase the Deere, or hunt the Hare.' New College, Oxford, had a sundial and
a complete alphabet cut in box.

The reaction against topiary came with the eighteenth-century embrace of 'natural'
landscape. Alexander Pope famously pilloried the work of the 'garden tailor' in *The Guardian*
(then a periodical journal) and offered a mock topiary shopping list:

> *Adam and Eve in yew, Adam a little shattered by the fall of the tree of
> Knowledge in the great storm; Eve and the serpent very flourishing;
> St George in box, his arm scarce long enough, but will be in condition to
> stick the Dragon by next April.*

Topiary fell out of favour for the best part of a hundred years, eventually being revived by
the Arts and Crafts movement in the late nineteenth century. Although some of our most
famous topiary gardens, such as Levens in Cumbria or Packwood in Warwickshire, were

first planted in the late seventeenth century, they were restored during the nineteenth, and much of their topiary represents nineteenth-century plantings. It is perhaps the fun and eccentricity of topiary that has made it so enduring, for instance, at the north London garden in which a privet hedge has been clipped to form the single word 'Arsenal'. Large topiary pieces are commonly executed in yew, but many other plants are suitable: privet was favoured in the sixteenth and seventeenth centuries, alongside box, cypress, bay, hawthorn and rosemary.

WILDERNESSES

IF YOU GO TO A TYPICAL seventeenth-century wilderness garden, such as the one that has been restored at Ham House in Surrey, you will find, just outside the main flower garden, a rectangular garden laid out in the form of what looks like a Union flag with a central circular clearing. Each of the lines of the 'flag' forms a straight grassy path, bordered each side by neatly clipped hedges, and with trees regularly and symmetrically planted to give shade. Within the triangles are smaller paths, flowers and a covered seat for reading. You may ask what this has to do with 'wilderness', at least in the sense that we now understand the word, and the answer is...nothing. The wilderness garden is one of those peculiarly English creations, fixed in time by the development of our language. You have to think of 'wilderness' in the biblical sense – a place of solitude, without inhabitants – just as a 'desert' for Elizabethans is not a sandy landscape, but 'somewhere deserted'. The wilderness garden was a place to be alone – to think, to read and reflect in privacy. Part of that privacy is being a little removed from the house, hence the location just outside the principal gardens.

The first wilderness garden in England was probably laid out in the 1580s at the royal palace of Nonsuch in Surrey. It was created not by a king, however, but by the garden lover Lord Lumley, whose father had bought the palace from Queen Mary I. Lumley had travelled to Italy and visited gardens there, so it is likely that he got the idea for a wilderness from the Italian *bosco*, or little wood, often marked by straight paths and high hedges. Why the English form was called 'wilderness' and not 'bosco' is a mystery. The gardens were uprooted by Oliver Cromwell's men, and precious few records remain. The first documentary record we have of a wilderness garden is at Blickling Hall around 1620. That

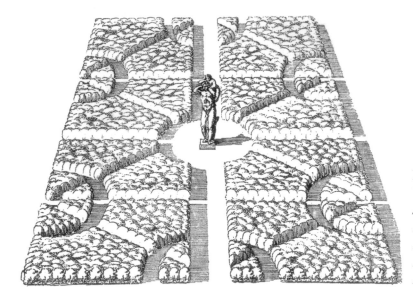

LEFT: *The plan of the
Wilderness at Wilton,
Somerset. If the statue
looks disproportionately
large, that may be because
the drawing was made by
its creator.*

too has since disappeared, though another was planted nearby in the familiar Union flag pattern in the early eighteenth century – restored later on a grander scale by the Victorians, and still there today.

The high point of popularity for wilderness gardens was the late seventeenth century. Although many survived into the eighteenth century, and acquired fashionably serpentine paths, they gradually fell out of favour. This was partly because their exact geometric forms and high hedges didn't meld well with the new flowing lines and openness of the landscape garden, and partly because their function was gradually becoming obsolete. The desire for privacy could be satisfied in different ways: when every lonely grove in the landscape now formed part of your garden, what need for a little hedged area a short step from the house? And when the gardens around the house began to merge with the wider parkland, that demarcation line on the edge of the main gardens, where the wilderness had previously been located, no longer seemed to exist. The examples at Ham House and Blickling are among the best in the country, though there's also a wonderfully irregular eighteenth-century version at Castle Howard in Yorkshire.

CHAPTER THREE

FLOWERS & GRASSES

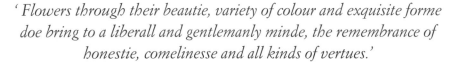

*' Flowers through their beautie, variety of colour and exquisite forme
doe bring to a liberall and gentlemanly minde, the remembrance of
honestie, comelinesse and all kinds of vertues.'*

JOHN GERARD

IN THE RENAISSANCE a garden where flowers were grown was sometimes called the 'pleasaunce' – literally, a place of pleasure or delight. In the prosaically minded eighteenth century this became more simply the 'pleasure ground'. The association between flowers and delight and pleasure remains, however, an abiding one. Gardeners grow flowers for their appeal to the senses and the imagination. Some have a rich symbolic life, and often these are amongst the oldest known to gardeners – roses and lilies, for example. Others are valued for their colour, scent or shape, or a combination of these qualities. But above all, flowers are the mark of a civilization that has progressed beyond the ordinary mechanics of existence, and that has developed a sense of beauty, of pleasure, and an appreciation of religious, ceremonial or personal symbolism. This makes flowers not the most ancient of garden elements, but perhaps the most redolent of meaning and significance.

Where did flowers come from? The question might seem an odd one, yet, as with so many elements of the garden, flowers have their own distinctive and sometimes fascinating history and geography. Before the Norman invasion of 1066, the word 'flower' did not exist in English. The Anglo-Saxon equivalent was *blostma* or *blosme*, which, like our 'blossom', denoted the

LEFT: *The herbaceous border at Hardwick Hall, Derbyshire. The stone wall with its elaborate finials dates to 1587, but the border itself is a 20th-century creation, inspired by Gertrude Jekyll.*

91

flowers that trees put out before they fruit. Flowers for the pre-Norman English were the natural blooms on trees and hedges, not those cultivated in gardens. Of course, the countryside wasn't the only place you could find them; many monasteries boasted a well-stocked garden, and in AD 795 the Emperor Charlemagne had issued a list of seventy plants, including roses and lilies, that he wished every town to cultivate. But the overwhelming majority of Charlemagne's plants, like those in the monastery gardens, were grown for food or medicine. For the ordinary Saxon or Frank the concept of cultivated flowers, or of a flower garden, simply didn't exist.

Flowers, then, entered the English garden, and the English language, with the Normans. Of course, the Normans didn't invent them. Their word, *flour*, developed from the Latin *florem*; and the ancestry of *florem* stretches right back to the ancient Aryan word *blhō*, which found its own way into English as the verb 'blow', meaning 'to come into flower'. The idea of flowers, then, comes to England from Aryan culture: from the ancient civilizations of India, Iran and the Fertile Crescent of the Middle East. This chapter will explore, among other things, how that long journey was made, and the impact it had on gardens around the world.

ABOVE: *A wild flower meadow at Crook Hall,
Durham, alive with poppies, thistles, cow parsley and
tall-stemmed native grasses.*

Grasses also owe much to the Normans, and this is particularly true of the commonest use of grasses in the garden: the lawn. This ancestry may seem surprising in something so quintessentially English. When the Normans arrived in England, however, they found a landscape with extensive forest cover. Where they came across a break or clearing in the forest, they called it *launde*, an old French word for 'land'. The word *launde* became part of medieval English, meaning simply 'an open space among woods'; there's one mentioned in Shakespeare's *Henry VI*: 'Through this Laund anon the Deere will come'. In a sense, then, the lawn (a corruption of *launde*) was originally defined by opposition – a lawn is 'not forest' – and, as we explore below, it would be several centuries before the lawn was valued in its own right.

RIGHT: *Rhododendrons have been brought to England from the Americas and Asia since the 18th century. This bloom comes from the gardens at Glendoick, Perthshire, whose creator Euan Cox went hunting for rhododendrons in Burma just after the First World War.*

THE BIRTH OF FLOWERS

GROWING FLOWERS FOR pleasure in the ancient world was the exception, not the rule. The very earliest garden elements were water, shade and privacy, often embodied in a tree-lined pool attached to a house or palace. In Mesopotamia (present-day Iraq) gardens were primarily orchards, providing fresh fruit for offerings to the gods: the words for 'orchard' and 'garden' were one and the same. In Ancient Egypt flowers were cultivated for specific uses: lilies were harvested and pressed to make perfume, poppies grown for their medicinal value. The symbolic qualities of flowers, however, began to be recognized. The lotus, for example, which opened in the morning and closed at night, was a symbol of rebirth. Indeed, lotus flowers were an important element in religious ceremonies, sometimes placed in the grave as a promise of new life. The Egyptian civilization was the first to import flowers, including cornflowers, irises and delphiniums.

Perhaps the first lovers of flowers were the ancient Greeks. Homer mentions many species, including violets, hyacinths, crocuses and narcissi. Nurseries for violets were established in Attica, and rose gardens were well known. The island of Rhodes was especially celebrated for its roses, which were sacred to the goddess Aphrodite. Flowers found their most powerful significance in sacred terms: Aphrodite was called the 'violet-crowned', and funerary flowers were by now a well-established tradition. The midsummer festival of Adonis encouraged the growing of flowers in pots. Adonis, in origin a vegetation deity, came to symbolize short-lived beauty. Around the time of his festival, flowers were grown in shallow containers: they quickly bloomed, but just as quickly died without constant watering, and at the festival's close their withered remains were ceremonially thrown into the sea. It's possible that this marks the beginning of container gardening: by Roman times observance of the festival was widespread, but the festival pots and urns remained on city terraces and balconies all year round. The Romans themselves imported many flowers from Greek gardens, though they also cultivated flowers already native to Italy, such as forget-me-nots, lilies and periwinkles. Like the Greeks, the Romans associated particular flowers with deities. Ovid expounded many of these associations in his poem *Metamorphoses*, which, among numerous stories, recounts how Narcissus fell in love with his own image in the reflected waters of a pool, and was metamorphosed into a flower; and how the youth Hyacinth was accidentally killed by his lover Apollo, and similarly transformed.

✦ FLOWER JOURNEYS

IN OUR SECTION ON flower gardens (see page 101) we explore how the use of flowers has developed in the English garden. First, however, it's worth noting that the great majority of flowers in our gardens are foreigners. Some of the oldest – and still the most popular – are natives of the Mediterranean and Middle East: the daffodil, the tulip, the iris and the lily. Many come from even more exotic locations. How did they arrive in our gardens?

More portable than animals – or, indeed, humans – flower seeds and bulbs have been passed from country to country for thousands of years, since the time of the Ancient Egyptians. The earliest flower journeys were almost certainly prompted by the religious associations already mentioned. The first recorded plant-collecting expedition set out in 1495 BC, led by the Egyptian Prince Nehasi in search of incense-bearing plants for use in temple ceremonies. Later motives for such expeditions included medicine, aesthetics and, of course, commerce. Ovid's *Metamorphoses* was one of the most popular literary works in medieval and Renaissance Europe, and his stories helped to establish a cult of symbolism for flowers and for gardens generally that has persisted to this day.

Travelogue of Popular Flowers

Below are the journeys made by some of the most well-known garden flowers, and the dates when they first arrived in Britain.

55BC	**LILY**	**ANCIENT EGYPT AND PERSIA**

The lily was grown by ancient civilizations across the Mediterranean basin and into Asia, but it was probably the Romans who introduced the flower to England. Japanese lilies were described by Englebert Kaempfer in 1690, and Chinese lilies first brought to Europe by the Abbé David in the late nineteenth century.

NARCISSUS **ANCIENT EGYPT AND PERSIA**

Cultivated by the Ancient Egyptians, the narcissus was probably brought to England by the Romans.

IRIS (*see opposite, left*) **ANCIENT GREECE AND EGYPT**

Cultivated in Minoa and Egypt during the second millennium BC, the iris may have reached English gardens through the Roman occupation, or possibly from French monastic gardens of the fifth to tenth centuries.

C. 1100 **CARNATION** **ANCIENT GREECE**

First described by Aristotle's pupil Theophrastus in the third century BC, carnations were used by the Romans to flavour drinks, and this long-lived tradition may have led to the flower being introduced to England by crusaders returning from Palestine. Carnations were not grown in America until the late eighteenth century.

1563 **GERANIUM** **SOUTH AFRICA**

The first geranium in Europe was brought from South Africa by John Tradescant the Younger in 1563. Seeds were sent to America in 1760, and Thomas Jefferson, following his time as US ambassador to France, also carried plants back with him in 1789.

1573   HYACINTH   MIDDLE EAST

Hyacinths were valued by the Ancient Greeks and Romans, but not cultivated by other Europeans for many centuries. A German doctor, Leonhardt Rauwolf, collected samples when he visited Turkey in 1573, and thereafter they spread to the rest of Europe.

1573   TULIP   PERSIA

Tulips were cultivated in Persia from at least the twelfth century, and in Turkey from the fifteenth century, but did not reach Holland (the country with which they have become most associated) until 1593. They may have arrived in England earlier, during the 1570s, introduced by Huguenot refugees. By 1642 they were being grown in the United States.

1596   ANEMONE   ANCIENT GREECE

The anemone was an important flower for the ancient Greeks. The word comes from the ancient Sanskrit verb 'to breathe'; the goddess Anemone was daughter of the wind. The wood anemone is a native plant, but *Anemone coronavria*, the Garden or Poppy Anemone, was first brought to England from the Middle East in the late sixteenth century: John Gerard, who called it the 'wind-flower', described several varieties in 1596.

1637   LOBELIA (*see above, right*)   AMERICAS AND SOUTH AFRICA

Lobelia cardinalis is a native of North America, and was brought to Europe by John Tradescant the Younger in 1637. The popular bedding plant *Lobelia erinus* was introduced from South Africa in 1752.

1656   **RHODODENDRON** (*see below*)   **CHINA**

Rhododendrons and azaleas grow naturally in various parts of the world, but were probably first cultivated by the Chinese. The first rhododendron in England was grown in the Lambeth garden of John Tradescant in 1656. The American azalea was brought to England in 1734.

1699   **SWEET PEA** (*see opposite, left*)   **SICILY**

A Sicilian monk, Francisco Cupani, first sent seeds of the sweet pea to Robert Uvedale, the headmaster of Enfield Grammar School, in 1699. A hundred years later the poet John Keats began his education as an eight-year-old in the same school. The flower was originally called the 'sweet-scented pea', but was described by Keats in one of his earliest poems as the 'sweet pea', and his version of the name stuck.

1732   **PHLOX**   **NORTH AMERICA**

Phlox paniculata, or garden phlox, was introduced to Europe from America by the apothecary James Sherard in 1732.

1789   **DAHLIA** (*see opposite, right*)   **MEXICO**

The first dahlias in Europe were grown by the Abbé Cavanilles in the Royal Botanical Gardens in Madrid from seeds sent from Mexico. He named the plant after Andreas Dahl, a distinguished Swedish botanist. Dahlias were brought to England shortly afterwards by the Marchioness of Bute, though the early arrivals all died.

1790   **HOSTA**   **CHINA AND JAPAN**
Hostas were first described to Europeans by Englebert Kaempfer, a doctor for the Dutch East India Company, in 1712, but the first variety to reach England was probably *Hosta ventricosa*, which came from China in 1790.

1795   **CHRYSANTHEMUM**   **ANCIENT CHINA**
Although cultivated in China for 2500 years, the florist's chrysanthemum was grown in Europe only after arriving on a French merchant's ship in 1789. It was first sold by English nurserymen in 1795.

1795   **PETUNIA**   **ARGENTINA**
Petunias were first sent to England from Argentina by John Tweedie, a Scottish gardener who emigrated to Buenos Aires at the age of fifty to begin a new career as a plant collector. He 'discovered' many plants, including the pampas grass.

1826   **VERBENA**   **ARGENTINA**
The first verbena to be grown in England was discovered in Argentina in 1826, but the originals of the popular bedding varieties were sent to England by John Tweedie during the 1830s.

1870   **BUDDLEIA**   **CHINA**
Seeds of the *Buddleia davidii* (butterfly plant) were first sent to Europe from China by the French missionary Abbé Armand David in 1870. Buddleia is actually named after another botanical priest – the Essex vicar Adam Buddle (1660–1715).

BULBS, BANKERS & TULIPOMANIA

AS THE TRAVELOGUE BOX on the preceding pages shows, the great age of flower journeys began in the late sixteenth century. There are many reasons for this. One is that Renaissance Europe was more politically stable than it had been in the Middle Ages. Communications were better, and travel somewhat safer – certainly for diplomats, who were some of the most reliable early plant collectors. Sir Henry Wotton (1568–1639), the British ambassador in Paris, sent some of the first orange trees to England, while Ogier de Busbecq (*c.* 1521–1598), ambassador of the Hapsburg Emperor Ferdinand I to Constantinople, dispatched numerous Middle Eastern plants, including tulips, to western Europe. A new breed of gardener emerged to take advantage of these networks of communication: the Tradescants are the best examples in England, exchanging plants and seeds with fellow collectors nations apart. Perhaps most important was the opening up of trade routes both within Europe and between Europe and the wider world – the Americas to the west and the spice routes to the east. Mercantile communities in London, Antwerp and other large ports were often the first recipients of new plants.

The rise and fall of 'tulipomania' is an index to the new Europe. The original habitat of the flower seems to have been the Pamir-Alai and Tien-Shan mountains of Kyrgyzstan, many of which remain unexplored today. Who exactly first brought tulips to western Europe we don't know, but credit is usually given to Ogier de Busbecq. In 1554 he found them growing near Adrianople in Turkey. The Turkish name for them was *lalé*, derived from the Persian *laleh*, which is still a common girl's name in Iran. But either because they were displayed in a turban, or because he was told they resembled a turban, de Busbecq thought they were called *tuliband* – the Turkish word for 'turban'.

From Constantinople the new flowers travelled to Vienna, Paris, London and Amsterdam. The Dutch were not the first recipients, but they were among the most enthusiastic. By 1600 tulip bulbs were already fetching high prices. The flower was a status symbol. At first an aristocratic rarity, within a couple of flower generations (six years for the tulip) there were just sufficient number of them to be more widely accessible, without losing their earlier cachet. By 1630 the Dutch were successful international traders, with numerous overseas colonies including New Amsterdam (later New York). Dutch merchants were enjoying unprecedented prosperity. That prosperity found its unique outlet in the appreciation of tulips. They were sold at auction (which encouraged even higher prices) and later on the stock exchange.

Tulipomania itself was a commodity speculation of 1634–7, a classic stock-market bubble that had little to do with gardens, and everything to do with people making money. Although it is difficult to equate prices accurately, it's certainly true that the price commanded for a single tulip bulb in 1637 could have bought a smart house in Amsterdam. The very rarest 'sports' (mutations) fetched prodigious sums. Unfortunately, these sports were not caused by the skill of breeders, but by a

ABOVE: *A garden of the late 15th century, planted with flowers typical of the period, including roses and lilies.*

virus that caused the flower to 'break' (change colour). The action of the virus was entirely unpredictable, and the market therefore entirely unstable. The inevitable crash came in the spring of 1637, and left thousands of investors with huge debts and no compensation. It has even been suggested that the loss of New Amsterdam to the British some twenty-five years later, and its reincarnation as New York, can be traced back to the disastrous tulip crash of 1637.

FLOWER GARDENS

FLOWER GARDENS ARE a physical terminus for the journeys we have been tracing. Although the medieval *hortus conclusus* is sometimes misleadingly described as a flower garden, the range of flowers planted was limited: violets, columbines, lilies, roses and irises (though more colour would have been provided by the blossom of fruit trees and the flowers of medicinal herbs). In medieval descriptions of gardens, flowers do not in fact rate very highly. An important ideal was the garden of love described in the thirteenth-century allegorical work *Romance of the Rose*. Here the reader is conducted through fruit trees, spices, ornamental trees, shaded lawns, streams and wells before flowers get any mention. Growing flowers for pleasure required the economic prosperity of the sixteenth century, but it also required a fuller palette of colours, hence the importance of the new arrivals. The historian William Harrison described some of them in 1577: 'It is a world also to see how manie strange hearbs, plants, and annuall fruits are dailie

brought unto us from the Indies, Americas, Taprobane, Canarie Iles and all parts of the world… There is not almost one noble man, gentleman or merchant, that hath not great store of these floures.' Harrison was probably getting ahead of himself a little here, but it is true that within fifty years of his account, English gardens were filling up with flowers. Most of the thousand plants described in John Parkinson's great plant book of 1629 were meant for the 'garden of pleasure' or flower garden. Parkinson even devoted separate chapters to English flowers and to 'Outlandish flowers' (foreign imports). The first true flower gardens were found in the gardens of seventeenth-century gentry and nobility, the flowers planted in the 'open work' of knots, or in beds bordered with low hedges. There was a particularly fine one at Wilton (Wiltshire).

We don't normally associate the English landscape garden of the eighteenth century with flowers. Inviting grassy parkland right up to the walls of the house does not, on the face of it, leave much room for garden ornament, floral or otherwise. Flower gardens, however, were maintained, sometimes in rather less spectacular fashion or in slightly out of the way locations. As in earlier centuries, they were predominantly the preserve of women, and in some large gardens it is still possible to come across an area with a name like 'My Lady's Garden', which may well date from this period. The poet William Mason is sometimes credited with bringing flowers back into the garden around 1770 when he carved serpentine and kidney-shaped flower-beds into his lawn at Nuneham Courtenay in Cambridgeshire.

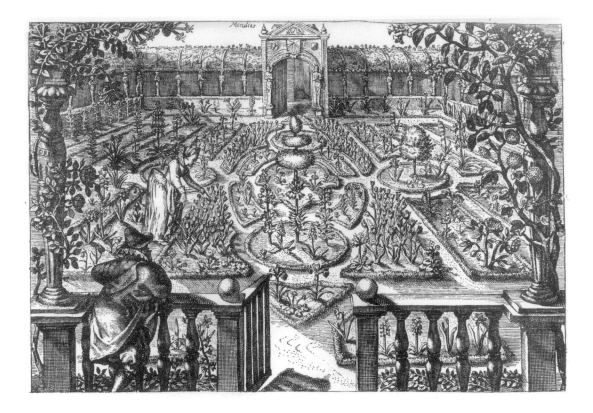

LEFT AND ABOVE: *Two gardens illustrated by the Dutch artist Crispin de Pass in his book* Hortus Floridus *(1614). The one on the left is titled 'Spring Garden', and the one above 'Summer Garden'. They show the development of the new flower garden in the early 17th century.*

Something like a modern flower garden can be seen in the work of Humphry Repton, who in his modification of the natural landscape style started planting neat little beds and erecting trellises and picket fences around the house. 'Flower gardens,' he informed his clients, 'on a small scale may, with propriety, be formal and artificial; but in all cases they require neatness and attention.' Repton's small, proper flower gardens were eclipsed by the next great wave of flower imports: the new bedding plants from the southern hemisphere (see pages 109–12). These required heated greenhouses and stupendous resources of manpower, but they enabled entire gardens to be carpeted with flowers of the gaudiest hues.

The reaction came with the forthright (and still widely read) William Robinson, who launched a broadside against summer bedding in *The English Flower-Garden* (1883). For Robinson the English flower garden was simply a garden near the house with 'a variety of form of shrub and flower'; without unnatural lines and divisions; and with hardy plants that didn't

LEFT: *The gardens at Gravetye Manor, West Sussex, were designed by William Robinson in the late 19th century in pursuit of a natural English garden.*

CHAPTER THREE:
FLOWERS AND
GRASSES
❁

need hothouses to keep them alive through the winter. Robinson was famous for the manner of his departure from his first gardening job: opening the windows of the greenhouses at night and putting out all the fires. But his vision of gardens 'planted with large drifts of softly coloured perennials' was very influential, both on gardeners such as Gertrude Jekyll (see page 38) and Norah Lindsay (1876–1948), and on flower gardens today. Jekyll herself was one of the twentieth century's most important influences on the use of flowers in gardens. Her gardens were (and are) ravishing compositions of artfully gradated colour, and her books, such as *Colour in the Flower Garden*, sold by the thousand.

COTTAGE GARDENS

THE COTTAGE GARDEN is a curious hybrid: on the one hand a sentimental ideal, nursed by Victorian paintings such as those by Myles Birkett Foster and Helen Allingham; on the other hand, a prosaic reality for thousands of ordinary cottage dwellers, who quietly got on with planting their gardens – and not especially joyfully at that.

The word 'cottage' is medieval, but it was about 500 years before anyone thought of using it in a favourable sense. Cottage gardens throughout those centuries were almost entirely utilitarian, containing vegetables, chickens and perhaps a pig. During the eighteenth century, as the cultivation of flowers slipped down the social ladder, factory workers began to turn at least part of their gardens over to pinks, carnations and auriculas – sometimes to wondrous effect; but the rural cottage garden remained a larder, a hedge against starvation. Ironically, it was perhaps the Enclosure Acts of the later eighteenth century – so ruinous to the country poor with the loss of common grazing lands – that helped to foster the 'traditional' cottage garden. When the verge between the cottage and the road was no longer grazed by animals, it could be fenced in to create a front garden – invaluable space now that the commons had been lost. Animals might be kept at the rear of the house; vegetables, herbs and even some flowers at the front.

The practical ethos of the cottage garden is to grow what you can where you can. There is no plan and no design principle. The plants are hardy and readily available, not bought, but exchanged as seeds with neighbours – hence the preservation of ancient flower varieties in such gardens. So it is that some of the twentieth century's most artful and aesthetically satisfying gardens owe a debt to an artless, unsophisticated predecessor.

It is, however, the sentimental ideal – the 'chocolate box' cottage garden – that has exercised the greater hold upon our imagination. Such gardens are always full of flowers in lush but not untidy profusion, which is why they find a place in this chapter. If you are searching for the influence of cottage garden planting, you might look at Gertrude Jekyll's Munstead Wood, or even at Beth Chatto's garden in Essex, with its emphasis on plants that can look after themselves. There was a brief vogue during the eighteenth and early nineteenth centuries for fake cottages or cottages *ornées*, erected in picturesque positions for aristocrats to sample the quaint pleasures of their tenants' lives. One of these – a veritable mansion built for the Duchess of Bedford – can still be seen at Endsleigh in Devon.

▦ PLEASURE GROUNDS

THE TERM 'PLEASURE GROUND' first appeared in around 1750, just as the landscape garden was really starting to take off. In a sense, a pleasure ground is simply the area that would have been the garden before the new landscape gardeners removed the old division between garden near the house and parkland beyond. Although in theory there was no division in landscape, in practice the area nearer the house was more particularly cared for, and did need a different name, even if 'garden' wouldn't do. The new landscapers were preoccupied with being natural – and what could be more unnatural than the old-fashioned word 'garden'? 'Pleasure ground' is a much more nebulous, idealistic name. It actually alludes to a classical ideal, the Vale of Tempe beside Mount Olympus, which was the resort of the gods and the most delightful, pleasing place on Earth. Tempe was the perfect model for a classically obsessed eighteenth century that wanted its landscape to be at the same time as natural and as ideal as possible.

Of course, art couldn't be kept out for long: by the end of the century Humphry Repton was recommending people 'to ornament the lawn with flowers and shrubs, and to attach to the mansion that scene of "embellished neatness", usually called a Pleasure Ground'. There can be few gardens more obviously unnatural than a 'scene of embellished neatness'. Pleasure ground, then, is a general term in the late eighteenth and nineteenth centuries for the area of garden between the house and the park, the line of division between the two often being a ha-ha. It gradually fell out of use in the early years of the twentieth century.

PLEASURE GARDENS

PLEASURE GARDENS ARE a lost form of mass urban recreation, which once enjoyed enormous popularity. Two things distinguish them from gardens open to the public today. One is that they came alive at night – certainly during their heyday in the eighteenth century – when they would be spectacularly illuminated. This meant that although pleasure gardens were often attractively planted, the trees, shrubs and flowers were not the visitors' primary interest: they came to see each other and to watch the entertainments staged by the proprietors. The other difference was their popularity. Owners of historic gardens today have to balance visitor access with the needs of conservation: an organization such as the National Trust will restrict the numbers of visitors to its most popular sites in order to protect against degradation of paths and so forth. By contrast, an eighteenth-century London pleasure garden simply could not function if it was not crammed with visitors; and if a proprietor did not get as many feet as possible on those paths, his business would soon close.

Many city pleasure gardens, whether in London or elsewhere, developed from tavern gardens. As their popularity grew, they began to be purpose built. The largest and most famous was Vauxhall Gardens in south London, which began life as the New Spring Gardens in 1661. By the mid-eighteenth century Vauxhall had an orchestra room in the form of a Greek temple, and an ornately furnished rotunda. The gardens were patronized by the Prince of Wales, and became immensely popular, not least for their musical performances: 12,000 spectators are said to have turned up for a rehearsal of Handel's *Music for the Royal Fireworks* – unfortunately without any fireworks, which were actually quite common at Vauxhall. Arbours within the garden contained fifty 'boxes' where patrons could dine on food that was proverbially expensive (a 'Vauxhall slice' was a sliver of ham through which you could read a newspaper). Each night the gardens were illuminated by oil lamps suspended from every available branch: in 1786 there were over 14,000 of them. Always notorious for prostitution, Vauxhall gradually slid into a tawdry decline, and the gardens eventually closed in 1841. Earlier rivals in Marylebone had closed in 1788, and at Ranelagh (a more up-market version across the river in Chelsea) in 1803. Provincial cities, such as Manchester and Liverpool, had their own versions. No pleasure gardens of the eighteenth century have survived to this day.

BEDS & BORDERS

BEDS

As ancient as gardens themselves, beds first appear in the old Teutonic languages, where a 'garden bed' and a 'place to sleep' have the same ancient, Aryan root, meaning a 'place dug out' or a 'lair'. Some of the first beds recorded in England are mentioned in a leechdom (Saxon herbal) of the tenth century, which describes a *wyrtbed* – *wyrt* being the word for a root or plant, still used in names such as St John's wort.

Raised Beds

Raised beds were a feature of medieval gardens from at least the eighth century, and were almost certainly inherited from Roman gardeners. The soil would be contained with boards, bricks or a woven lattice of coppice poles. We sometimes think of raised beds being seat-high, rather like a turf bench, but in fact they might be only a few inches above the adjacent paths. One explanation for this is that good soil was a luxury that might have to be carried to the site of the garden from elsewhere: the height of the bed above the path would be determined simply by the amount of new soil laid down. In medieval gardens the beds would be devoted to herbs and vegetables, less often to flowers. During the seventeenth century they gradually fell out of favour, as ornamental

beds – whether planted with hedge plants or flowers – increased in size, and as the norm for garden visitors changed from looking at the flowers, to looking down on them. When the garden is viewed firstly from the upper floors of the house, raising flower beds by a few inches is hardly worth the effort. Within the kitchen garden, however, the utilitarian value of raised beds ensured their retention: indeed, you may still come across kitchen gardens today laid out with raised beds dating from the early nineteenth century.

Carp Beds

If you visit a restored seventeenth-century garden, such as that at Westbury Court in Gloucestershire, you will find very narrow flower-beds edged with low hedging, such as box. The earth within these beds is raised to form a ridge running from end to end, with specimen flowers, such as tulips, planted along it. Known as carp beds, the origin of the name is obscure. The

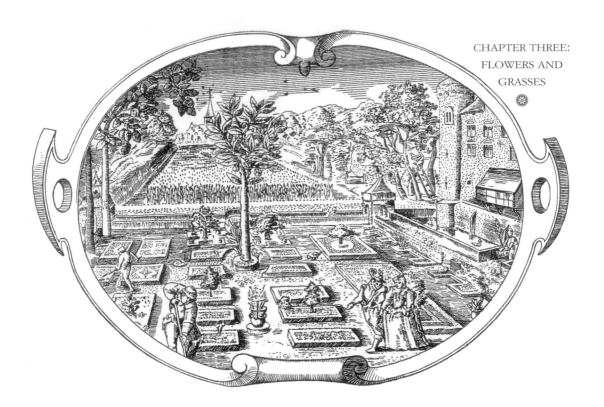

simplest and likeliest explanation is that the ridge recalls the distinctive domed back of the carp fish. When we remember that carp would have been kept as a convenient source of food in fish-ponds close to the gardens from medieval times until around the eighteenth century, it is easy to see how the association might have been made.

BEDDING

THE TERM 'BEDDING' is a contraction of 'bedding out', which refers to tender ornamental plants (typically non-native) that are raised in a green-house, then planted out in the warmer months of summer. The practice of using bedding plants became popular because it seemed to permit more variety and colour in the flower garden. Conducted on a large scale, however, it requires a lot of money for plants and labour, and not much regard for 'natural' gardening. It was first started, appropriately enough, in the royal gardens of pre-Revolutionary France, where money and labour were no object, and beds might be entirely changed mid-season. The following piece of advice, given by an anonymous writer to English gardeners in 1825, may still ring true for some today: 'The beauty of the flower-garden, in the summer season, may be heightened by planting in beds some of the most freely-flowering young and healthy greenhouse plants. Where there is an extent of greenhouse, a sufficient quantity of plants should be grown annually for this purpose, and should be sunk in the beds about the middle or end of May.'

Two practical points helped bedding out to become popular. One was the development of effective greenhouses, which Joseph Paxton

RIGHT: *Carpet bedding in the faithfully restored South Parterre at the Rothschild house, Waddesdon Manor in Buckinghamshire.*

(designer of the Crystal Palace for the Great Exhibition of 1851) did much to advance in the mid-nineteenth century. The other was the availability of new, exotically coloured annuals, many from South and Central America and South Africa. These combined with the typical Victorian delight in colour to result in a passion pursued with perhaps more enthusiasm than discrimination in many gardens.

At first the idea was to create 'masses' of bright colours – a concept developed by John Caie, the Duke of Bedford's gardener, in the 1830s – and within twenty years 'massing' had become a familar part of large gardens. Variations, such as three-dimensional bedding, were explored. This involved laying soil over a pyramid or cone of rubble, then 'bedding' it with suitably bright colours of flower or foliage. Gardeners began to turn against bedding in the last decades of the century, as advocates of 'natural' and 'woodland' gardening, such as William Robinson, inveighed against the garishness and artificiality of the high Victorian flower garden: 'pastry-work gardening' was Robinson's dismissive comment. Another factor was the cost of labour, which was considerably higher at the end of the nineteenth century than it was at the beginning. In public parks and gardens, however, massed bedding remained popular right through to World War I and beyond: many councils still practise it in a reduced form, and publicly owned parks remain

ABOVE: *The 'Conservative Wall' at Chatsworth, Derbyshire, built by Joseph Paxton between 1842 and 1850. No sooner was it complete than Paxton began the Crystal Palace in London.*

its common home. To see a truly spectacular example of Victorian bedding during the summer months you should visit Lyme Park in Cheshire or Waddesdon Manor in Buckinghamshire.

CARPET BEDDING

CARPET BEDDING IS the laying out of bedding plants in patterns that resemble a carpet in their intricacy of design. The first attempt at this was made by John Fleming, the Duke of Sutherland's gardener at Cliveden in Buckinghamshire, in 1868. He loyally created his employer's name in foliage plants such as echeveria and sedum, and the result was given the name 'carpet bedding' in a review by the *Gardeners' Chronicle*. The innovation quickly became popular, especially in public parks, where designs that incorporated the names of towns, significant dates, and even animals and human figures might entertain the parkgoers. Ironically, despite the name 'carpet',

it became more usual to plant these designs on raised beds – or, indeed, in three-dimensional forms – where they could be more easily viewed. Higher-minded individuals were, of course, appalled by the practice. William Robinson said, quite truthfully, that it degraded flowers into crude colour without natural form. The designer William Morris loathed carpet bedding: 'Another thing also much too commonly seen is an aberration of the human mind, which otherwise I should have been ashamed to warn you of. It is technically called carpet-gardening. Need I explain further? I had rather not, for when I think of it even when I am quite alone I blush with shame at the thought.'

As with other forms of massed bedding, carpet bedding fell out of fashion in the early 1900s, though again it remained popular in public parks, and can still be seen in many of them (albeit on a less monumental scale) today.

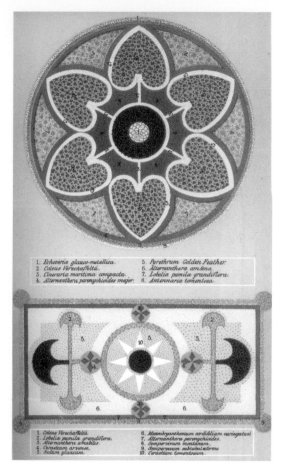

MOSAICULTURE

THE TERM 'MOSAICULTURE' was first used in France during the 1870s to describe the creation of geometric and emblematic shapes in flower-beds. At first these were imitations of seventeenth-century designs, but soon they were elaborated into vast pictorial narratives: in Italy, Biblical tableaux were especially popular. Some were created in England – for example, an enormous bed in the shape of a butterfly at Crystal Palace in 1875 – but they were more popular on the Continent, until the demise of the fashion around the time of World War I.

ABOVE: *Two more examples of Victorian carpet bedding designs. These give some idea of just how elaborate and striking contemporary design had become.*

RIBBON BEDDING

THE PRACTICE OF planting narrow lines of highly coloured bedding plants in parallel rows beside paths is known as 'ribbon bedding'. It was first established at Trentham in Staffordshire during the 1850s, and became a popular variant on Victorian bedding schemes.

◈ BORDERS

ALTHOUGH THE WORD 'border' is medieval, it wasn't used in relation to gardens before about 1600. One of the earliest mentions of the term is in the poem *Muiopotmos* (1591) by Edmund Spenser, which describes a butterfly fleeing from a jealous spider into a garden:

> *There he arriving, round about doth flie,*
> *From bed to bed, from one to other border,*
> *And takes survey with curious busie eye,*
> *Of everie flowre and herbe there set in order*

ABOVE: *Purple and yellow borders flanked by yew hedges in the gardens at Wallington, Northumberland, laid out in the early twentieth century, and restored by the National Trust.*

The association of 'border' and 'order' was actually quite long-lived, and when the straight lines of seventeenth-century formal gardens fell out of fashion, the border seemed destined to share their fate. Joseph Addison, arguing for the new informality, asked for 'a wonderful profusion of flowers...*without* being disposed into regular borders and parterres'. Gardeners often talk about 'herbaceous borders', and although 'herbaceous' simply means, as it sounds, 'relating to herbs', the phrase 'herbaceous border' is conventionally understood as a border of flowers and flowering shrubs that are perennial (come up year after year). In fact, when early nineteenth-century gardeners first started using the phrase 'herbaceous border', they meant the kind of border that seventeenth-century formal gardens used to have, and that had to some extent disappeared following the censure of writers such as Addison. The border came back into favour when the Victorians developed an interest in garden history and re-created what they thought were 'historic' garden borders with plants that included a number of perennials. (Whether they were right or not is another matter.)

As the planting of exotic annuals in beds became fashionable, critics such as the vociferous William Robinson began to eulogize the border and its perennials as a superior alternative. Thus the convention set in that beds should be planted with annuals, and borders with perennials. So the herbaceous border is actually a by-product of Victorian gardening fashions. It finally came into its own towards the end of the nineteenth century, when Gertrude Jekyll began laying out her gardens at Munstead Wood, and publishing the first of many books on flowers, their colours and their use (above all) in borders. For Jekyll, a border was a complete aesthetic experience:

> *The planting of the border is designed to show a distinct scheme of colour arrangement. … at the near or western end, there are flowers of pure blue, gray-blue, white, palest yellow and palest pink; each colour partly in distinct masses and partly inter-grouped. The colouring then passes through stronger yellows to orange to red. By the time the middle space of the border is reached, the colour is strong and gorgeous. Then the colour-strength recedes in an inverse sequence through orange and deep yellow to pale yellow, white and palest pink, with the blue-gray foliage. But at this eastern end, instead of pure blues, we have purples and lilacs … the whole border can be seen as one picture, the cool colouring at the ends enhancing the brilliant warmth of the middle.*

A Jekyll border could be pretty substantial – one at Munstead Wood was 14 feet (4.3 m) deep and 200 feet (60 m) long – so reproducing it in the ordinary back garden was not really feasible. But this detailed, minutely orchestrated attention to colour and form brought Jekyll's flower borders triumphantly to life, and her model and methods remain hugely influential. Her work can still be seen at Hestercombe in Somerset, and at the Manor House, Upton Grey in Hampshire.

❖ BOWLING GREENS & BOWLING ALLEYS

FEW GARDENS TODAY possess a bowling green or alley, yet bowls is, of all sports, the one that has had most impact on the English garden. It is an ancient game: the oldest green (or alley, as it was then known) still in use was laid at Southampton in 1299. We know little of the provision made in medieval gardens for bowls, though the game was certainly played in public gardens around London and must have been very popular: four medieval and Tudor monarchs banned it. The story of Sir Francis Drake (*c.* 1540–96) refusing to fight the Spaniards until he had finished his game of bowls is entirely characteristic; one of the reasons given for the royal prohibition was that bowls kept people from the archery they ought to be practising in case of war. The alternatives were discussed by William Lawson in a guide for Jacobean gardeners: 'To have occasion to exercise within your Orchard: it shall be a pleasure to have a bowling Alley, or rather (which is more manly, and more healthfull) a paire of Buts, to stretch your arms.' ('Buts', now spelt 'butts', were targets for practising archery.)

The bowling alley was the earlier playing surface, and was, as its name suggests, longer and narrower than today's bowling green. The first greens were laid in the mid-seventeenth century, and may have coincided with the end of Oliver Cromwell's Commonwealth and of Puritan disapproval of the game. Bowling alleys experienced some competition at the time of the Restoration from the game of *pallemaille*, brought over from France by the returning court. This involved striking wooden balls with mallets similar to those used in croquet, and was played on a dry alley covered with earth and powdered shells. One of the earliest such alleys in England was laid in St James's Park – hence the modern name, Pall Mall. The diarist Samuel Pepys was breathless with excitement at seeing the brother of King Charles II play there, and couldn't restrain a little surge of national pride: 'the green of our bowling alleys is better than any they [the French] have'.

The eighteenth-century delight in English grass was doubtless a factor in the game's renewed popularity. A guide from the early years of the century declares, 'a bowling green is one of the most agreeable compartments of a garden and when 'tis rightly placed, nothing is more pleasant to the eye. It demands a beautiful carpet of turf very smooth and of a lovely green.' Indeed, in the first half of the eighteenth century bowling greens were a near-universal feature of English gardens. By the early nineteenth century, however, they were starting to acquire an unfashionable reputation: bowling greens began to disappear from the gardens of private houses, and to reappear in those of private clubs. These proliferated in the early twentieth century, when many greens were also laid in public parks.

In the gardens of pubs and taverns, bowling greens could be found from the Middle Ages right through to the mid-eighteenth century, but many of these were lost to nineteenth-century building developments. You are unlikely to find original bowling greens in the grounds of historic houses, but you can still track down the location they once occupied: look for a long, narrow, level piece of ground, possibly enclosed, and not too far from the house.

LAWNS

AS WE HAVE ALREADY seen (page 93), 'lawn' derives from 'laund', a Norman word used to describe an open space or clearing in woodland. The humanist Sir Thomas Elyot described just such an area in 1538: 'a place voyde of trees, as a laune in a parke or forrest'. A laund might be found in a deer park, a clearing through which a hunt would pass. For several hundred years, then, the laund or laune was a part of designed landscapes, particularly forest and parkland, often associated with hunting, and with the pleasure provided by landscape. It is this parkland heritage that is important. The lawn as we know it – that clear area of grass close to the house – came into existence only when parkland approached the house. For the moment of its birth we have to look to the English landscape garden of the eighteenth century, and to its love of parkland. Philip Miller, who published a *Gardeners' Dictionary* in 1733, described the lawn thus: 'Lawn is a great Plain in a Park, or a spacious Plain adjoining to a noble Seat… As to the Situation of a Lawn, it will be best in the Front of the House, and to lie open to the neighbouring Country and not pent up with Trees.'

This is not to say that earlier gardeners – whether medieval, Tudor, or seventeenth-century – did not grow grass in their gardens: only that they did not call it a lawn. Grass was highly valued in medieval gardens. As Albertus Magnus, one of our very earliest garden authorities, wrote around 1260, 'the sight is in no way so pleasantly refreshed as by fine and close grass kept short' – a boon for the sore eyes of monastic scribes. The medieval 'flowery mead' is actually a later fiction (see pages 123–5), but there is no doubt that medieval gardeners knew how to keep their grass: Albertus Magnus's instructions for laying turf could be followed profitably today.

The gardens of the sixteenth and seventeenth centuries used grass in square plots, a relic of medieval practice, but added extended walks and alleys – the latter for bowling, which was enormously popular (see pages 118–19). Francis Bacon's advice echoes that of Albertus Magnus – appropriately enough, as both were philosophers and alchemists: 'The green hath two pleasures – the one because nothing is more pleasant to the eye than green grass finely shorn, the other because it will give you a fair alley in the midst.' The key phrase is 'finely shorn'. The mowing of grass was hard but very expert work, and the finish obtained was just as fine as those offered by modern lawn mowers. Grass in a country house garden might be mowed every three days to keep its pristine appearance, and in the late seventeenth century was often referred to as 'carpet ground' or 'carpet walks'.

ABOVE: *The classic English lawn of the 19th and early 20th century is a perfect foil to flowers. This example is at Crook Hall, Durham.*

These prototype lawns were the envy of Europe. Indeed, the French gardening authority Antoine-Joseph Dezallier d'Argenville observed despairingly in 1709 that 'in England...their grass plots are of so exquisite a beauty that in France we can hardly hope to come up with it'. By the beginning of the eighteenth century, when the old parkland launds began to invade the garden, the cultivation of grass was one of long-established perfection. It was this national triumph that provided the ideal setting for the eighteenth-century country house. 'A Regular

 # LAWNMOWERS

THE LAWNMOWER WAS invented in 1830. Called the 'Budding', after its designer Edwin Budding, it was based on machines developed to shave the nap from newly woven cloth. Other rival inventors were quick to produce their own versions. These early mechanical mowers were either pushed by hand or, in the case of larger models, dragged behind a pony. Their popularity grew slowly, but by 1870 they were almost universally accepted by English gardeners. The chief gain was not in quality, but in the saving of time and labour. It was notoriously difficult to obtain a close, even cut with early-nineteenth-century lawnmowers. But their speed was devastating. An acre of lawn that might have provided a team of scything gardeners with a morning's work could be cut by one man with a machine and a pony in five minutes.

The first self-propelled mowers were developed around 1900. The earliest were short-lived steam versions, quickly superseded by the petrol-engined models, whose descendants still buzz and roar about our lawns today.

LEFT: *The Georgian Terrace at Muncaster Castle,
Cumbria, laid out in the late 18th century.*

Parterre, or Lawn, stript of all those Decorations, of tonsur'd Plants with which the Gardeners
have heretofore loaded them, when smooth and even, and of a proper Proportion, strikes the
eye with a certain Reverence and Grandeur scarcely expressible,' decreed the gardening writer
Stephen Switzer in 1742. Although there were detractors – Humphry Repton, towards the end
of the century, was not alone in pointing out the absurdity of houses stranded in a sea of lawn
– this setting had the great advantage of being relatively simple and cheap to maintain
compared to the smaller compartments and numerous gravelled walks of the previous
century.

Almost nine out of ten English gardens still possess a lawn, many of them planted within
the last half century. The typical English back garden lawn probably owes its presence to a
Victorian ideal of the perfect garden, which has gradually filtered down to the smallest
suburban spaces.

▦ MEADOWS & MEADS

ALTHOUGH POPULAR ACCOUNTS of medieval gardens talk about the 'flowery mead',
this is actually a later invention – a phrase coined by twentieth-century garden historians.
Medieval writers do mention meads: there is one described by Bartholomew de Glanville in
the thirteenth century as 'y-hight [adorned] with herb and grass and flowers of diverse kind'.
Most medieval writers wrote in Latin, however, not English, and therefore used the Latin

word *pratum*. The English equivalent for those few who decided to use the vernacular was *medwa* or *medwe*, which eventually became 'meadow'.

A meadow was not, primarily, part of an ornamental landscape – as 'flowery mead' implies – but a field of hay to be cut for animal feed. A *pratum* would be more luxurious, more decorative and more recreational. The Italian writer Giovanni Boccaccio (1313–75) describes ladies seated on *un prato di minutissima erba*, which is usually translated as 'a lawn of the finest turf'.

Meads and meadows with their native flowers remained part of the agricultural landscape for centuries, but the idealized flowering versions begin to appear in poetry in the late seventeenth and eighteenth centuries. An early description comes from the poet William Collins (1721–59), who, according to his friend Dr Johnson, 'loved fairies, genii, giants, and monsters' – which might tell us how removed from reality the idea was.

In recent years the wildflower meadow has become popular. The roots of the fashion can be traced all the way back to the late nineteenth century, when 'wild gardens' were advocated by William Robinson as a reaction against the hothouse artificialities of the high Victorian garden. Robinson's 'wild gardens' weren't in fact especially wild: he sensibly described his method as placing plants 'where they will take care of themselves'. But this emphasis on self-supporting native plants, and disapproval of formal planting schemes, was influential. The true impetus for the creation of wildflower meadows has been the response of conservationists to the near-extinction of such meadows in their natural form. It's estimated that 98 per cent of these meadows have been destroyed in the past sixty years. No doubt the fashion for planting wildflower meadows in gardens will pass, but while it lasts, it makes a small but vital contribution to the maintenance of natural flora and to the wildlife they support. Wildflower meadows are not created without labour, for the simple reason that they require impoverished soil. Most gardens are too rich, and have to be leeched of nutrients before the native wild flowers will bloom.

ORNAMENTAL GRASSES

THE USE OF ORNAMENTAL GRASSES in gardens is a relatively modern development. During the late nineteenth century gardeners began planting things such as pampas grass from South America, or miscanthus from northeast Asia. They were encouraged by advocates of

HOW TO READ
AN ENGLISH
GARDEN
❋

RIGHT: *A woodland walk cut through bluebells and rhododendrons at Little Bowden, Berkshire.*

LEFT: *Ornamental grasses in the gardens at Waltham Place, Berkshire.*
BELOW: *A parterre of 'compartments', which is distinguished by being symmetrical about both the horizontal and the vertical axis.*

CHAPTER THREE:
FLOWERS AND
GRASSES

✦

'natural' planting styles, such as William Robinson and Gertrude Jekyll. However, the planting of ornamental grasses only gained widespread popularity during the late twentieth century, in imitation of their use by contemporary landscape architects and garden designers.

PARTERRES

A PARTERRE IS A FLAT, ornamental garden adjacent to the house, with regular beds often laid out in elaborate, scroll-like shapes that imitate the form of plants. The first parterre was created in box around 1580 by the French royal gardener Claude Mollet at the Château Anet. By the early years of the seventeenth century the French parterre had developed a distinctive, embroidered appearance – *parterre de broderie* – as seen at Fontainebleau and St Germain-en-Laye. A description by the contemporary French authority Jacque Boyceau (1580–1633) shows how important and various the ornamental aspects of parterres quickly became: 'Parterres are the low embellishments of gardens, which have great grace, especially when seen from an elevated position: they are made of borders of several shrubs and sub-shrubs of various colours, fashioned in different manners, as compartments, foliage, braidings, Moresques [Moorish designs], arabesques, grotesques, guill-oches [designs of braided ribbons], rosettes, sunbursts, escutcheons, coats of arms, monograms and devices.'

These elaborations soon arrived in England, and there were early and extensive versions at Wilton in Wiltshire. Around the middle of the seventeenth century, the gardener Thomas Hanmer gave his own account of the new creations: 'Parterres, as the French call them, are often of fine turf, but as low as any green to bowl on; cut out curiously into embroidery of flowers, and shapes of arabesques, animals, or birds, or feuillages [foliage], and the small alleys or intervals filled with several coloured sands and dust with much art, with but few flowers

129

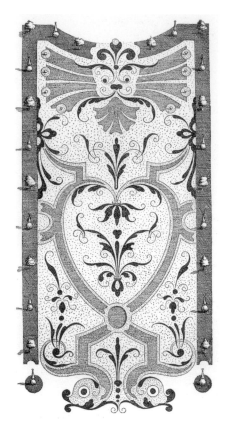

LEFT: *An early-18th-century parterre of cut turf punctuated with specimen flowers.* RIGHT: *A parterre de broderie, or embroidered parterre, in which the patterns are marked out with box, turf and coloured earth. This example comes from the early 18th century.*

in such knots, and those only as grow very low lest they spoil the beauty of the embroidery.' However, until the end of the seventeenth century the word 'knot' was in more general use than 'parterre'. It was then the gardeners London and Wise who, typically, codified just exactly what a parterre in an English garden ought to be. 'There's nothing,' they wrote, 'more ingenious belonging to a Garden, than the different Ways of marking out different Figures in a Parterre.' Just how many different ways and figures they were only too happy to expound:

> *Some Parterres are said to be imbroider'd; others partly imbroider'd, and partly Cut-work with Borders; a third sort compos'd of Grass-work only; a fourth made up of Imbroidery and Grass-work; a fifth only Cut-work; a sixth nothing but Cut-work and Turfs of Grass; a seventh of Cut-work of Grass and Imbroidery; an eighth whose Middle is all Cut-work, and the Border Imbroidery; a ninth on the contrary, whose Borders are all Cut-work, and the Middle Imbroidery; and lastly another sort, whose Middle is partly Imbroidery, partly Cut-work and green Turf, with Borders of Turf and Cut-work.*

RIGHT: *A parterre of 'compartiments', probably laid out in coloured earths, and with a pool at its centre.*

The use of those coloured sands mentioned by Hanmer are also explained: 'Some curious Persons, to please the Eye the better, put Things of different Colours into these Branch-works and Flourishes, such as powder'd Tile, which is red; beaten Charcoal and Iron-Filing, which are black, and the yellowest Sand they can get…'

London and Wise planted many such parterres beside country houses during the early eighteenth century. They were and are, however, incredibly laborious to maintain: they require a great deal of clipping, and the sands and powders have to be relaid after every rainstorm. Advocates of the landscape garden were soon railing against the parterre's artificial intricacies, and the various forms fell out of fashion by the end of the century.

The parterre was rediscovered by the Victorians, not least the designer W.A. Nesfield (1793–1881), who adapted many seventeenth-century patterns at gardens such as Witley Court in Worcestershire. Today there are few, if any, original seventeenth-century parterres in existence. Most in England are restorations or re-creations of the nineteenth century and after. There is a good example at Drummond Castle in Perthshire, but the best versions are still to be found in France.

ROSARIES

A ROSARY IS A shrubbery (see below) devoted to roses. They were first planted in medieval and Tudor gardens, but fell out of favour in the seventeenth century. During the eighteenth century they enjoyed a partial revival as an unusual form of the newly fashionable shrubbery: the Empress Josephine had a particularly fine example planted for her in Paris. Rosaries were really rediscovered, however, by Regency and Victorian gardeners with an interest in historical planting: there is a good example at Battersea Park, London. There are, of course, strong associations between rosary gardens and Catholic devotion to the Blessed Virgin Mary, for whose intercession the Rosary is recited, and many twentieth-century rosary gardens have been planted as places of meditation.

LEFT: *The gardens of Muncaster Castle in Cumbria were first laid out in the late 18th century, and their dramatic hillside location exemplifies the picturesque fashion then in the ascendant.*

CHAPTER THREE:
FLOWERS AND
GRASSES
❀

SHRUBBERIES

'SHRUB', MEANING A 'bush' or 'lytyll tree', is an ancient Saxon word that was in fairly common usage by the Middle Ages. But the term 'shrubbery', applied to flowering shrubs planted together for ornamental purposes, does not occur until the eighteenth century. It's almost as if people didn't think small bushes grouped together were worth looking at until that date. The first shrubberies were probably planted by Philip Southcote and William Shenstone in their respective gardens at Woburn Farm in Surrey and The Leasowes in Warwickshire. It might be no coincidence that both Shenstone and Southcote were aiming at a kind of rustic landscape, in which the humble shrub would not be beneath their notice. In fact, the eighteenth-century shrubbery was often a place for displaying exotic plants – the far from rustic new arrivals, particularly from America – and it quickly became fashionable. One anonymous writer in 1756 described the creation of shrubberies as 'a national disease'. For others they were the height of luxury: a visitor to Hagley (Worcestershire) in 1777 described how he 'lingered through the pleasant shady bowers of an elegant and extensive shrubbery, breathing ambrosial gales from every surrounding bush and flower'. Inevitably, there was some adverse reaction. 'Curse on the shrubbery's insipid scenes!' wrote Richard Paine Knight, an advocate of rugged picturesque landscape. But the shrubbery was here to stay.

During the nineteenth century, fashion turned away from the 'mixed shrubbery' to a system of 'mass planting', where similar species were grown together. Over time, however, the stronger, more rapacious plants, such as cherry laurel and Portuguese laurel, tended to take over, creating the dark, thick Victorian shrubbery of popular fiction. Charles Dickens's friend Wilkie Collins, credited with inventing the detective novel, found shrubberies a perfect place for his malefactors to lurk in; Sherlock Holmes tracked down criminals in them – even Dracula

Now think of the gaiety of a shrubbery!
ANONYMOUS EIGHTEENTH CENTURY WRITER

Curse on the shrubbery's insipid scenes!
RICHARD PAINE KNIGHT

RIGHT: *A medieval turf seat, supported by wooden boards.*
OPPOSITE: *Rhododendron in the gardens of Glendoick, Perthshire.*

chose a shrubbery as a hiding-place. These associations of dark, damp gloominess might help to explain the shrubbery's decline in popularity during the twentieth century, though lack of space was probably another factor. Today English back gardens average around 23 x 100 feet (7 x 30 m), which simply isn't big enough for a flourishing shrubbery. To see a shrubbery in its full, colourful, exciting state requires a visit to restored eighteenth-century gardens, such as those at Painshill in Surrey.

✸ TURF SEATS

TURF SEATS ARE ONE of the best-known features of the medieval garden. One of the earliest records of them comes from the thirteenth-century saint and philosopher Albertus Magnus, but they remained popular for centuries. William Lawson, in a book written for the 'Country Housewife' in 1618, tells her that 'banks and Seats of Cammomile, Penny-royall, Daisies and Violets, are seemly and comfortable'. They are actually quite difficult to maintain in good condition, and, despite Lawson's advice, not always comfortable to sit on (especially after rain). Their presence in so many early paintings of gardens tells us therefore something about the high value placed by medieval and Tudor gardeners on turf, as opposed to wood or stone. Probably this had something to do with the delight in green grass already noted in medieval writers – as a respite for the eyes, and as a general relief from interior work. In the simplest form of seat, turf would be placed on top of soil held in place by boards, bricks or wattle; though some were turfed vertically as well. As Lawson's words indicate, it wasn't simply grass that was employed – flowering herbs were also popular.

CHAPTER FOUR

FOOD

Vineyards, orchards, gardens and such enclosed plots are the flowers,
starres and paradises of the earth.
RALPH AUSTEN

GROWING PLANTS FOR FOOD is the most basic form of gardening – indeed, the only form of gardening for the early English gardener. Despite its long history, what we think of as a 'kitchen garden' is a comparatively recent creation. It is typical of the scientifically adventurous seventeenth century that it not only welcomed enormous quantities of new plants into Britain, but also found new ways of developing productive gardens. Most productive gardens, however, date from no earlier than the nineteenth century. Gardeners through history have seldom felt overwhelmingly tender towards their kitchen gardens, which tend to be torn down and rebuilt without compunction. In consequence, it is generally the latest, Victorian walled gardens that are the survivors. Today, however, gardeners and garden visitors do feel genuinely attached to the old kitchen gardens. One of the great ironies of garden visiting is that now we are no longer burdened with the need to grow our own vegetables, we have become fascinated by the places where the work was done. The free time that we would have spent digging the allotment is instead spent visiting the kitchen gardens where our forefathers did their digging. In this chapter we will look at the various elements of the productive garden, and some associated areas, such as vineyards and hop gardens, and the physic or medicinal garden.

LEFT: *Vegetables growing in the gardens at Sheepdrove Farm, Berkshire.*

KITCHEN GARDENS

KITCHEN GARDENS AND their contents are subjects of huge and varied interest, well able to fill a book in their own right. They have a quite precisely limited history of approximately 300 years: seldom in existence before 1650, and rarely seen in complete working order after 1950. As attractions for garden visitors, their history is also exceptionally limited. For centuries, those who visited a garden simply to see how its produce was grown were very few and far between. It is only in the past twenty years or so that we have learnt to visit, enjoy and even love these little vegetable factories. Many have been restored in the course of those twenty years, but they are still a tiny fraction of the number that once flourished and are now lost. The great majority of kitchen gardens still standing date from the nineteenth century: we should add at once that by 'still standing' we don't mean 'still cultivated'. If you visit a kitchen garden today, it will probably be Victorian in origin, and will probably stand a little further from the house than its first incarnation and a little nearer than any eighteenth-century predecessor. The reasons for all this are explained below.

The kitchen garden is really a Jacobean invention. We should remember that for the ordinary medieval (or, indeed, Tudor) household the garden was the kitchen garden – there was no other. The term 'kitchen garden' came into general use in the early years of the seventeenth century. You might think this reflected a sudden surge of interest in the growing of vegetables. Actually, it was something rather opposite: a sudden surge of interest in growing flowers. This meant that gardens were now more clearly divided in purpose than they had been previously.

We have already noted just how many new flowers were introduced to England in the late sixteenth and early seventeenth centuries. Those new introductions led the gardening writer William Lawson to advise his readers: 'it is meete…that we have two Gardens: a garden for flowres and a Kitchin garden'. The development of the kitchen garden is a consequence of the development of the flower garden. This is not to say that some people weren't using the words earlier – just that it hadn't reached common parlance. The earliest example we have found dates from 1374 and refers to a 'kechengardyn' at Teynham in Kent. Teynham was known above all for the cultivation of fruit trees – cherries and apples in particular – which flourished here as nowhere else in England. Perhaps the name 'kechengardyn' was introduced to distinguish the area devoted to lowly vegetables from Teynham's more usual orchard enclosures.

No garden stands still, but kitchen gardens in particular often change their location. A typical large country house and estate, such as Chatsworth in Derbyshire, is a good example. The earliest

map of the gardens, from 1617, shows no separate kitchen garden at all. In 1694 a walled kitchen garden was created by London and Wise just a few yards north of the house, in an area now grassed over beneath the great Cascade. Kitchen gardens were close to the house in the seventeenth century because it was convenient for the kitchen staff; and in an age when just about every part of the garden was a walled enclosure geometrically laid out, there was no aesthetic reason to put the kitchen garden anywhere else. In the 1740s the Chatsworth kitchen garden was moved to a new location a little further from the house. It was still only 130 yards (120 m) away, but it was on the south side, no longer in the shadow of the house itself, and had warm, south-facing walls to help ripen fruit. It meant that the gardens beneath the north front could now be united in the new, open, 'natural' style – probably on the advice of the designer William Kent.

ABOVE: *Seakale and rhubarb pots in the kitchen garden at Nanhoron, Gwynedd. These have been used for centuries to blanch the vegetables inside, making their leaves whiter, crisper and more tender.*

In the 1760s Capability Brown was employed to re-landscape the grounds at Chatsworth, and, as was the case with many estates at the time, he moved the kitchen garden right away from the house to an entirely new site – a complex of 7 acres (2.8 hectares) about 1½ miles (2.4 km) away in the park. The reasons for the move were really twofold. First, the solid, geometric block formed by the walled kitchen garden clashed with the broad open sweep of the typical eighteenth-century, pasture-dominated landscape: this utilitarian area did not form part of the newly fashionable vision of English Arcadia. Second, the smell was unacceptable. The cultivation of tender fruit and vegetables, such as melons, cucumbers and pineapples, became very popular in the eighteenth century; pineapple growing particularly could almost be described as a mania. But all these exotics needed heat to be grown successfully, and the commonest source for that heat was rotting animal dung, which needed to be turned regularly. Not the sort of activity a country house owner wanted nearby.

The kitchen garden at Chatsworth remained in its distant parkland site right up until the twentieth century. At other estates it might have moved nearer to the house again in the nineteenth century, though not as near as it originally stood: perhaps, say, within 800 m (half a mile). This time the reason for the move would have been simply one of convenience. It wasn't that kitchen gardens had suddenly become more aesthetically delightful – in fact, during the nineteenth century they were often miracles of utilitarian productivity. But they could be hidden from view behind a screen of trees, as many were, and they didn't need to be several miles away to avoid the smell of dung. Just as importantly, cooking for the estate's owners, visitors and workers was much simpler without a lengthy trip for the raw ingredients. Humphry Repton made this practical point in typically orotund style at the close of the eighteenth century: 'Convenience and comfort, I confess, have occasionally misled modern improvers into the absurdity of not only banishing the appearance but the reality of all comfort and convenience to a distance; as I have frequently found in the bad choice of a spot for the kitchen-garden.'

Chatsworth's kitchen garden, however, remained marooned in parkland. Its fate, and that of many other nineteenth-century kitchen gardens, was decided not by aesthetics, nor indeed by horticultural developments, but by war and economics. Chatsworth had around eighty gardeners before World War I, but only twenty after it. War killed many gardeners, but it also broke the tradition of country house service. Better wages were available in factories, and there were fewer country families who could afford to match them – especially after the hike in taxes and death duties in 1919. Between the two world wars, Chatsworth's kitchen gardens, and many others throughout England, fell into terminal decline. In the late twentieth century came the final irony: the productive garden as a leisure interest. The Chatsworth gardens were relocated to a new, smaller site on the edge of the ornamental gardens, about 400 yards (350 m) from the house, and opened to visitors in 1994.

Chatsworth gives us an idea of the general history of the kitchen garden, and where we should expect to find such a garden when we visit other country estates. But there are other factors to look out for as well.

Size

THE SIZE OF kitchen gardens varies considerably. One of the earliest plans for a vegetable garden is that of the monastery at St Gall in Switzerland (*c.* AD 800): it occupied about 480 square yards (400 square metres) – less than a tenth of the size of a modern football pitch. Chatsworth's in the eighteenth century contained 7 acres (2.8 hectares) – about five football pitches – and was typical of the grandest estates of the period. Blenheim's was of a similar size, while Queen Victoria's kitchen gardens at Windsor occupied all of 31 acres (12.5 hectares) – or 25 football pitches. In general, the very largest kitchen gardens date from the nineteenth century, and the 'average' country house kitchen garden was around 1½ acres (0.6 hectares) – about one football pitch.

RIGHT: *The kitchen garden at Chatsworth,
Derbyshire, in its latest location, within sight
of the house.*

SHAPE & ORIENTATION

THE USUAL SHAPE for kitchen gardens is a square or rectangle, which suits the linear arrangement of the various beds. However, there are variations: the occasional oval kitchen garden has been built, and several hectagonal or even octagonal variants. Humphry Repton designed a number of hexagonal kitchen gardens in the early nineteenth century. The usual orientation for a kitchen garden is based on giving fruit trees the maximum amount of sunlight. This typically produces a square facing not quite south – more like south-south-east – which means that the sunniest wall gets full sun a little before midday.

ENCLOSURE

WE TEND TO THINK of kitchen gardens as being walled, and in fact most of them are. However, the Elizabethan version – sometimes called the 'cook's garden' – might instead be hedged with hawthorn. Walls were reserved for wealthier, more prestigious households. Kitchen garden walls have tended to get higher over the centuries. The chief reason for this is that as the technology for glasshouses developed, and they were built to greater and greater size, so the walls against which they were built had to become correspondingly larger. Unless the garden you visit belongs to an especially grand estate (such as Blenheim in Oxfordshire), any kitchen garden with walls over 15 feet (4.5 m) high will probably belong to the nineteenth century.

A few kitchen gardens are double-walled, which means that they have a second wall surrounding the usual boundary wall. This additional perimeter could provide more space for the ripening of fruit trees. However, the reason for a second wall probably owed more to security and convenience. The dirty and smelly melon grounds (see page 140) were usually located outside the main kitchen garden, and placing a wall around them both screened the area from the delicate sensibilities of owners and visitors, and ensured that no one could steal their valuable produce.

Walls are, of course, a vital aspect of fruit production: they store the warmth of the sun's rays (especially if they are made of brick rather than stone), and reflect it back upon the trees trained against them. The extravagant kitchen gardens built by London and Wise at Melbourne Hall in the early eighteenth century included free-standing fruit walls facing south to perform precisely these functions.

Most kitchen garden walls are straight, but if you build them in zigzags or undulating curves, you can in theory increase the number of trees trained on them. Serpentine, zigzag or

crinkle-crankle walls were popular in the late eighteenth century in East Anglia and on the south coast. They probably owed their presence to foreign influence. Those on the south coast were often built by Napoleonic prisoners of war (there are several around Lymington in Hampshire), but their East Anglian cousins speak more of Flemish ancestry. They don't actually make fruit ripen faster, but their shape makes them structurally more stable than straight walls, which means they can be built more thinly, with fewer bricks – an attraction after the brick tax of 1784.

Heated walls, in which small fires on one side of the wall send hot air through flues to warm plants on the other side, were an innovation of the eighteenth century, and reasonably common throughout the period. During the nineteenth century they were adapted to carry pipes of hot water, rather than hot air, which made for a better distribution of heat. But they remained very labour intensive (sometimes requiring round-the-clock refuelling), difficult to manage, and only erratically productive. By the end of the nineteenth century they had largely fallen out of favour.

BEDS

PERHAPS THE ONE consistent characteristic of the kitchen garden is the shape of its beds. These have always been linear and geometric because that is the most productive arrangement. They have, however, moved up and down in the world. Medieval and Tudor gardens had raised beds, wide enough for a gardener on either side to touch hands, with the narrow intervening paths doubling as irrigation channels. These were the norm for hundreds of years, and only fell out of favour in the eighteenth century – partly due to the inconvenience of a path that had to carry both water and human feet, and partly due to the development of more sophisticated watering systems. Hotbeds, a development of the seventeenth century, are described on page 149.

GARDENERS

A ROUGH RULE of the kitchen garden is that you need two gardeners for every 1 acre (0.4 hectares). In practice it is not quite so clear-cut; staff working elsewhere on the estate might be sent to the kitchen garden in a busy week, and vice versa. To take one example: during a typical week at Oxburgh Hall in Norfolk in 1850, there were twenty-one staff working in the grounds, twelve of whom were in the kitchen garden, which was only a little bigger than an acre. Many kitchen gardens remain in disuse precisely because of the numbers of full-time staff required. One typical National Trust property, with gardens of 40 acres (16 hectares), has not yet fully restored its 4-acre (1.6-hectare) kitchen garden because it would have to double its present complement of gardeners in order to do so – an onerous financial burden.

PRODUCE

TO CATALOGUE THE changing range of vegetables and fruit grown in the kitchen garden would fill many hundreds of pages, so here we offer just a brief outline of the principal types of produce. The first myth to dispel is that the medieval diet was barbarically limited, a year-round monotony of peas and turnips, and that garden produce was correspondingly banal. Take the following medieval recipe for a salad:

SALAT

Take parsel, sawge, garlec, chibollas [a type of leek], onyons, leek, borage, myntes, porrectes [an unknown leaf], fenel, and ton tressis [cress], rew, rosemary, purslarye [purslane]; lave, and waishe hem clene; pike hem, pluk hem small with thyn honde, and mynge hem wel with rawe oile. Lay on vynegar and salt, and serve it forth.

Here is a dish of fourteen vegetables and herbs, which would not disgrace a twenty-first-century kitchen. Of course, this would not be daily food for every villein and cottar, but all these plants grew in the medieval garden. A fifteenth-century manuscript of 'herbys necessary for a gardyn' includes no fewer than 110 plants, from 'Alysaundre' (*Smyrnium olusatrum*, a herb eaten like celery) to 'Vervey' (vervain, or *Verbena officinalis*). Among the plants new to the medieval garden would have been carrots, lettuce, parsnips and turnips.

The agricultural writer Thomas Tusser (1524–80) gives a full list of vegetables for a garden of the mid-sixteenth century. He includes forty-three 'seeds and herbs for the kitchen'; twenty-

RIGHT: *The kitchen garden at Rofford Manor,
Oxfordshire: timeless in appearance, but developed
from a wilderness in the past twenty years.*

one 'herbs and roots for sallets and sauce'; and nine 'herbs and roots to boil or to butter'. He also reminds us that tending the vegetable garden was very much the woman's responsibility:

> *In Marche and in Aprill, from morning to night:*
> *in sowing and setting, good huswives delight.*
> *To have in their gardein or some other plot:*
> *to trim up their house, and to furnish their pot.*

For the Elizabethan vegetable garden we have the following account of the poor man's plot in 1577 from the contemporary historian William Harrison:

> *A poor man…thinketh himself very friendly dealt withal, if he may have an acre of ground assigned unto him, wherein to keep a cow, or wherein to set cabbages, radishes, parsnips, carrots, melons, pompons [pumpkins], or such like stuff, by which he and his poor household liveth as by their principal food, sith they can do no better.*
>
> *Such herbs, fruits, and roots also as grow yearly out of the ground, of seed, have been very plentiful in this land, in the time of Edward I, and after his days; but in process of time they grew also to be neglected, so that from Henry IV till the beginning of Henry VIII, there was little or no use of them in England, but they remained either unknown or supposed as food more meet for hogs and savage beasts to feed upon than mankind. Whereas in my time their use is not only resumed among the poor commons, I mean of melons, pompons, gourds, cucumbers, radishes, skirets [water parsnips], parsnips, carrots, cabbages, navews [a type of brassica], turnips, and all kinds of salad herbs – but also fed upon as dainty dishes at the tables of delicate merchants, gentlemen, and the nobility, who make their provision yearly for new seeds out of strange countries, from whence they have them abundantly.*

If anything, the growth in 'new seeds out of strange countries' accelerated after Harrison's time. An early seventeenth-century edition of John Gerard's *Herball* lists no fewer than

RIGHT: *Kale growing in the organic garden at Sheepdrove Farm, Berkshire: a beautiful, showy vegetable that is also exceptionally nutritious.*

187 culinary plants grown in England, including some of those new arrivals. Potatoes were among them. First introduced to Europe from Peru by the Spanish, they probably reached England in the late sixteenth century. Kidney beans arrived in the first quarter of the seventeenth century, while runner beans were brought to England from Virginia by John Tradescant in 1633. The latter were first grown as ornamental climbers, and valued for their scarlet flowers – before someone realized that they were also rather tasty.

A typical kitchen garden in the eighteenth century would have included beds for artichokes, asparagus, beets, cabbage, carrots, cauliflowers, celery, cucumbers, kidney beans, leeks, lettuce, marrows, onions, peas, potatoes, radish and spinach, plus a whole range of salad herbs. Melons and pineapples would have been grown in hotbeds (see page 149) outside the main garden. The chief addition to the Victorian kitchen garden was the tomato – introduced to Britain from America in the sixteenth century, but not commonly grown in kitchen gardens until the late nineteenth century. There were few entirely new vegetables in the period, but the range of cultivars expanded enormously, and new technology enabled people to cook with a variety of fresh vegetables all the year round.

SPECIALIST AREAS & TECHNIQUES

INEVITABLY, THE INTRODUCTION of new and often exotic plants – especially those that disliked the chilly English climate – required the use of new growing techniques and environments, and some of these are outlined below.

CUCUMBER GROUND

CUCUMBERS WERE KNOWN in England in the middle ages. During the sixteenth and seventeenth centuries they were grown in hotbeds (see below), but as kitchen gardens increased in size in the eighteenth century cucumbers were allocated their own special ground. Victorian gardeners used to keep them straight by growing them inside long glass cylinders borrowed from lamps.

FRAMES, GLASSES & CLOCHES

GLASSES AND CLOCHES were introduced to English gardens in the early seventeenth century. Early versions, large enough to cover a single plant, were shaped like bells, and were probably by-products of the Renaissance glass industry. Hand-lights, of a similar size but made from several smaller pieces of glass, were in use by the end of the seventeenth century. Frames date from a similar period, and consisted of a wooden frame with panels of glass large enough to cover an entire bed. A cold frame is simply an unheated frame, unlike those versions placed on top of hotbeds (see below).

HOTBEDS

A HOTBED IS a hollow bed filled with animal dung and covered with a layer of top soil. Bacteria from the decomposing dung created heat, which enabled tender plants such as melons and cucumbers to be raised. The dung had to be turned several times before adding the topsoil in order to make sure the bacteria were present throughout the bed. This was a dirty and smelly task, which is one reason why hotbeds were often made outside the main kitchen garden. The first instructions for making a hotbed were given by the writer Thomas Hill in 1577, though the technique was known to both Roman and medieval gardeners. The heat from the dung could reach levels sufficient to kill plants, so it had to be carefully monitored. On the other hand, the heat lasted only a month or so; after that, fresh dung would have to be added to the sides of the bed to maintain the temperature. The unpleasant business of maintaining a hotbed is recorded in 'The Hot-Bed's Advice to a Certain Gardener', a poem by the actor David Garrick (1717–79), which ends with the couplet:

> *Be quiet, Brother, wisely think,*
> *The more we stir, the more we stink.*

MELON PITS

ALSO KNOWN AS a 'melon stove', the melon pit was a hotbed devoted to the raising of melons.

Eventually it became known as the 'forcing ground' or 'forcing pit', as the range of vegetables forced (grown earlier than the climate would otherwise permit) expanded far beyond just melons. The forcing pits were often covered with frames (rather like extended cold frames), so this area of the kitchen garden might also be known as the 'frame yard'.

PINEPITS

ALSO KNOWN AS a 'pineapple pit', a pinepit was a hotbed for growing pineapples. Unlike the usual hotbed, the pinepit was filled with tanner's bark, a by-product of the tanning industry, which converted animal hides into leather by steeping them in an infusion of an astringent bark, such as oak. The waste bark, at the end of the process, was known as 'tanner's bark', or simply 'tan', and it fermented, producing a gentle but consistent and continuous heat invaluable for the kitchen gardener. This was a Dutch innovation of the seventeenth century which reached England in the early eighteenth century. Tanner's bark continues to produce a steady heat for up to six months – far longer than animal dung – so was ideal for fashionable, but particularly troublesome exotics, such as pineapples. The pinepit would also be covered with a frame to ensure that the air temperature was consistent with that of the soil.

LEFT: *An Elizabethan garden of raised beds, watered with an early pump.*

✱

▦ Bee Gardens

Gardeners have been keeping bees in England since at least the Middle Ages. The familiar square wooden hive was developed in the late nineteenth century, but for hundreds of years before then, bees were housed by their keepers in straw skeps. Deriving from the Anglo-Saxon word for 'basket', a skep was woven in a distinctive, inverted cone shape. This was universally popular, as William Lawson commented in 1618: 'straw-hives are in use with us, and I think, with all the world, which I commend for nimblenesse, closenesse, warmnesse, and drynesse'. Most were kept in the open, raised off the ground on wooden or stone benches or stands, and protected from the rain with a straw hackle (roof). Wordsworth had a bee stand in his garden at Dove Cottage in Grasmere, Cumbria. In colder or upland areas the skeps might be housed in bee boles – niches in a thick garden wall, with a lintel or sometimes an arched top – to give protection from wind and rain. They are most common in Devon, Cornwall, Cumbria and Lancashire, but can be found in gardens elsewhere. Packwood House in Warwickshire has a wall with thirty boles dating from the mid-eighteenth century. Occasionally more substantial wooden hives were built, and the writer John Evelyn owned a transparent version. He had received this from 'that most obliging & universally Curious Dr. Wilkins', a don at Wadham College, Oxford, who built 'Transparent Apiaries…like Castles & Palaces…adorn'd with variety of Dials, little Statues, Vanes &c'. Wilkins had inserted little panes of glass into his hives so that the bees could be seen within. Charles II later paid a special visit to inspect the transparent hive in Evelyn's garden, much to its owner's gratification. One of the great advantages of Wilkins's hive was that honey could be removed without killing any bees – a process we take for granted today, but honey and wax could not be harvested from a skep without killing its inhabitants. The usual practice was to weigh the skeps at the end of the summer. The medium-weight skeps would be left to stand, as there would be just enough honey inside to keep the colony alive through the winter. The lightest and heaviest skeps were taken by the keeper – the lightest because there would be insufficient honey to sustain the colony, so it would die anyway; the heaviest because the keeper would lose too much honey to the colony. The skeps would then be either immersed in water or engulfed with a sulphurous smoke, killing the bees, and the honey and wax removed.

The term 'bee garden' has been in use since at least 1609, when Charles Butler published his treatise on bee-keeping called *The Feminine Monarchie*. Bees forage for flowers within

RIGHT: *A sheltered stone bee bole with a straw skep at Culross Palace, Fife, probably dating from the early 17th century.*

Store of Bees in a dry and warm Bee-house, comely made of Fir boards to sing, and sit, and feed upon your flowers…make a pleasant noyse and sight.
WILLIAM LAWSON

about 2 miles (3 km) of their hives, and advice has been given on what to plant near a colony of bees since Roman times: thyme and violets are enduring favourites.

Bee houses usually date from the nineteenth century, and were built to shelter the new wooden hives. There is a ten-sided Victorian bee house at Hall Place in Berkshire (now an agricultural college).

CHERRY GARDENS, GROUNDS & YARDS

CHERRY GARDENS HAVE usually taken the form of orchards planted by fruit farmers, particularly in Kent. Within the ornamental or pleasure garden, however, cherries have enjoyed two quite different periods of fashion: one in the seventeenth century, and another in the 1890s and after. The wild cherry, *Prunus avium*, is native to Britain, and the ancestor of later cultivated sweet cherries. The Romans were partial to cherries, and brought their own varieties. The word 'cherry' itself is a medieval one, inherited from the Normans: the Anglo-Saxon cherry tree was *Ceris beam*, and was grown in monastery gardens in the Dark Ages (fifth to tenth centuries). English cherries have been an important early summer fruit since medieval times: the fourteenth-century poet William Langland describes early summer as 'cherry-time'. They continued to be cultivated in monasteries up to the Dissolution (1536–9). The monastery at Norwich had a 'cherryyerd' alongside its *pomerium* (apple orchard), as did the monastery at Ely. Although Henry VIII destroyed the monasteries, he at least encouraged the growing of cherries: in 1533, the year his divorce from Catherine of Aragon finally came through, Henry allowed his 'fruiterer', Richard Harris, to import new varieties of sweet cherry from Flanders for an orchard at Teynham in Kent. In the decades that followed, Kent became the centre of cherry cultivation: the fruit was taken by boat to London, and sold by street sellers 'on the ryse' (a stick or stalk).

Cherries seem to have become rather fashionable around 1600, and many cherry gardens were established in the years that followed. The trees planted were the edible cherry: these were intended to be both productive and ornamental gardens, and they continued the great medieval and Tudor belief that orchards could be beautiful places. The increased interest in cherries at this time might also however have had something to do with the arrival of a new variety: the black cherry (*Prunus serotina*) from North America. The exact date of its arrival in Britain is not known, but John Tradescant was planting the species in the very prestigious garden at Hatfield in the early years of the seventeenth century. Another factor was royal approval: Queen Elizabeth I was well known for her love of cherries. When she visited Sir Francis Carew in August 1599, he was determined to give her fresh cherries despite the fact that the season would already have finished. He constructed a tent of damp canvas to cover a cherry tree in order to delay the ripening of the fruit, kept the canvas wet and removed it only 'when assured of her Majesties coming, so that she had cherries at least one moneth after all cherries had taken their farewell of England'. Carew also successfully grew the first oranges in England, so he knew his fruit. Thomas Cecil, brother of Hatfield's owner Robert, planted his own cherry garden of 119 trees at Wimbledon, one of the grandest houses of the period. Others were planted by the Countess of Pembroke, and the Duke and Duchess of Lauderdale.

Cherry gardens were popular within the city of London, often planted beside the river. Samuel Pepys visited one in Rotherhithe in 1664. As gardens developed in formality, the use of cherries became more spectacular. Moses Cook, a founder of the Brompton Nursery, planted whole avenues of them at the Earl of Essex's revolutionary late-seventeenth-century garden at Cassiobury in Hertfordshire. Some grew to 80 feet (25 m) high. 'They make a glorious show in spring,' wrote Cook, 'their white blossoms showing at a distance as though they were clothed with white linen.' It must have been a startling, modern sight.

Another reason for the abiding popularity of the cherry was its medicinal properties. The Elizabethan courtier Sir Philip Sidney coined the phrase 'a medicine of cherries', roughly equivalent to our 'sweeten the pill'. His contemporary William Langham, who wrote an important herbal called *The Garden of Health*, advised that 'the blacke sowre Cheries do strengthen the stomacke'; indeed, *Prunus serotina* was used for centuries for stomach complaints. William Temple, an innovative seventeenth-century gardener and an obsessive hypochondriac, would often eat 'thirty or forty cherries before meals' to be sure his digestion functioned properly.

❀

The cherry's second moment beneath the spotlight of garden fashion came in the 1890s, with the arrival of glorious blossoming cherries from Japan. This vogue differed from that of the seventeenth century in that it was part of a well-developed nursery industry, which ensured that the 100-plus new varieties of cherry were quickly available to ordinary gardeners. Many suburban gardens still possess the decrepit remains of cherries planted in the 1930s or earlier (flowering cherries tend not to live much past half a century, partly because the production of such exuberant blooms exhausts the tree). The Edwardian Japanese flowering cherry garden at Kingston Lacy in Dorset has recently been restored by the National Trust.

FERME ORNÉE

FERME ORNÉE MEANS literally 'ornamented farm'. The word *ferme* (farm) was used in the seventeenth century to describe a farm that was less dirty and more ideal or picturesque than usual. John Evelyn describes just such a *ferme* belonging to an uncle, whose meadows formed a 'goodly plaine or rather Sea of Carpet, which I think for evennesse, extent, Verdure, innumerable flocks, to be one of the most delightfull prospects in nature and put me in mind of the pleasant lives of the Shepherds we reade of in Romances & truer stories'. This idealized pastoral world was one of the mainsprings of the *ferme ornée*, which appeared in the eighteenth century. The other was the new theorists of the landscape garden – men such as Batty Langley, Stephen Switzer and Thomas Whately – who saw the bounds of the new gardens stretching far beyond those of the old. As Switzer put it, agriculture and gardening were 'unavoidably mixed'. The new gardening had reached out to appropriate the old parkland: why shouldn't it do the same with the farms? Batty Langley describes an ideal extended garden passing seamlessly from fruit garden to plantations to flower garden, 'and from thence through small Inclosures of Corn, open Plains, or small Meadows, Hop-Gardens, Orangeries, Melon-Grounds, Vineyards, Orchards, Nurseries, Physick-Gardens, Warrens, Paddocks of Deer, Sheep, Cows, &c. with the rural Enrichments of Hay-Stacks, Wood-Piles, &c.' If Langley's list seems exhaustive (or exhausting), it shows the extent to which the landscape garden had begun to appropriate other kinds of landscape that once upon a time had been distinct. There is a moment in the early eighteenth century when it seems that just about anything can be made into a garden. The *ferme ornée* is one consequence.

LEFT: *One of William Shenstone's streams at The Leasowes, Warwickshire: now recovering from years of neglect, but still offering glimpses of an ideal 18th-century landscape.*

CHAPTER FOUR:
FOOD

❋

The best-known *fermes ornées* were those of Philip Southcote at Woburn Farm in Surrey, and William Shenstone at The Leasowes in Warwickshire. As a Catholic, Southcote was barred from public office and, indeed, from more or less any other lucrative career. In 1733, however, he married the Dowager Duchess of Cleveland, who at 70 was just over twice his age, with a not unattractive dowry of £16,000. With that fortune Southcote in 1734 bought his farm, and began planting. Southcote initially said he simply wanted 'a walk all around my Farm', but over the years Woburn became something far more elaborate. The best description is that of Thomas Whately in 1770. The estate extended to 150 acres (60 hectares), of which 35 acres (14 hectares) was a highly ornamented pleasure ground. Southcote's 'walk', with its ornamental trees, shrubs and flowers, extended from the pleasure ground to encircle the farm. It was, as Whately said, 'the means of bringing every rural circumstance within the verge of a garden' – just as Langley and Switzer had foreseen – and composed a kind of Arcadian idyll, grazing cows and gardens mixed together.

Shenstone's The Leasowes was more slenderly financed than Woburn, but even more bucolic. He had inherited the estate in 1743, along with the somewhat meagre annual income of £300, which he regularly overspent in improving his garden, or *ferme*, as he preferred to call it. (He once worried that a path he was planting with flowers looked 'too like a garden'.) The Leasowes occupied a similar acreage to Woburn, but its agricultural qualities were never central to its appeal. Shenstone laid a circuitous walk past thirty-nine seats offering composed views of the surrounding landscape. Diversions were never far away: a Gothick screen, a Root House, an obelisk dedicated to Virgil, numerous springs and cascades… Along the way Shenstone provided epigrams for his visitors to read, some from his beloved Virgil, some of his own dainty and sometimes insipid composition: 'Here in cool grot and mossy cell, We rural fays and fairies dwell…' was carved into a stone tablet beside the Root House. The Leasowes was indeed one of the most visited gardens of the eighteenth century, and in that sense it fulfilled Shenstone's requirements. He once admitted, 'my *ferme ornée* procures me interviews with persons whom it might otherwise be my wish, rather than my good fortune, to see'. Although he craved celebrity, neither Shenstone nor his garden coped very well with it: obscene graffiti was scrawled on the walls and windows of the garden buildings; 'his hedges were broken, his statues and urns defaced, and his lawns worn bare', as a contemporary observed. Inevitably, the garden was at last closed to visitors. Shenstone died nearly bankrupt, and The Leasowes was sold to pay his debts. Woburn Farm lasted barely longer: Southcote outlived his duchess by little more than a decade, and within a century of the first plantings, the gardens had vanished.

Like so many ideals, the *ferme ornée* was forced to negotiate a rather unforgiving reality, without complete success. Today The Leasowes has been partly restored, and visitors can get some idea of how this Arcadian eighteenth-century tourist attraction might once have appeared.

Hop Gardens, Grounds & Yards

THE HOP GARDEN is not strictly speaking a garden at all, but a crop field. Probably its only ornamental form on a large scale would be within the confines of a *ferme ornée* (see above). Hops, which give beer its bitter flavour and help to preserve it, were introduced to England from Flanders in the late fifteenth or early sixteenth century. The plant is a climber, traditionally supported on hazel or ash coppice poles, and requires continual attention from the grower. Because of this, hops were originally grown in relatively small fields – hence the name 'hop garden' or 'hop yard'.

Despite early suspicions from the English (always slow to change their taste in beer), the hop gained popularity and became an important crop from the late sixteenth century. The first account of the widespread planting of hop gardens comes from the Elizabethan historian William Harrison, writing in 1577: 'Of late years also we have found and taken up a great trade in planting of hops, whereof our moory [marshy] hitherto and unprofitable grounds do yield such plenty and increase that there are few farmers or occupiers in the country which have not gardens and hops growing of their own'. Many country houses in the seventeenth and eighteenth centuries had their own small hop garden, as did many pub landlords, who brewed their own beer. The farming of hops expanded over the centuries to reach a peak in the late nineteenth century – also about the time that coppice poles were replaced by wires. The chief growing areas were Kent, Herefordshire and Worcestershire, and many place names in these counties retain references to the industry. The Kent hop gardens were picked each summer by tens of thousands of working-class Londoners, who would spend an entire month away from the capital. As domestic beer production decreased, so did the acreage devoted to hops, and the crop today is probably one-tenth the size of its late-nineteenth-century high point.

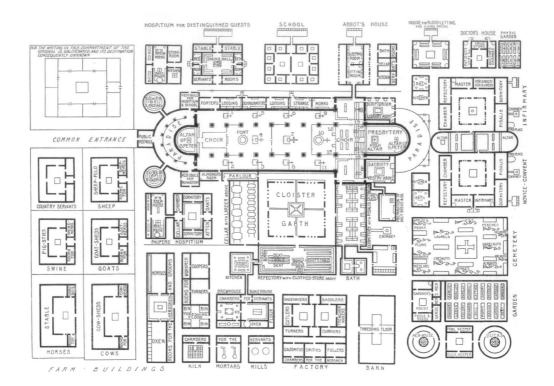

☖ ORCHARDS

ORCHARDS HAVE BEEN planted since gardens were first cultivated. In England they were especially valued by medieval and Tudor gardeners, who found them delightful places of recreation, as well as sources of food. In fact, for many centuries the words 'orchard' and 'garden' were synonymous. The Saxon *ort yerd*, derived from the Latin *hortus*, means simply 'garden' (or, even more literally, 'plant yard'); and right up to Elizabethan times a garden might be called an orchard, and vice versa.

The earliest plan of an orchard similar to those planted in the early Middle Ages belongs to the monastery at St Gall, where the orchard doubled as the monks' cemetery. A surprisingly wide variety of trees are indicated: apple, pear, mulberry, peach, plum, service, medlar, laurel, chestnut, fig, quince, hazelnut, almond and walnut. But this would also have been a place of quiet beauty

The principal end of an orchard is the honest delight of one
wearied with the workes of his lawful calling.
WILLIAM LAWSON

and reflection to evoke both the Garden of Eden and the Garden of Gethsemane. Indeed, our modern definition of the orchard as a place for growing fruit trees hardly does justice to its ancestry and variety of uses. Of course, fruit was important. One of the very earliest uses of the word 'orchard' in English, from around the time of Alfred the Great (849–99), describes it being filled with apples – *orcerdas mid aepplum afyllede*. Apples were probably the commonest fruit: a monastery orchard was often called the *pomarium* (apple place), even though apples were far from being the only thing grown. John Wyclif, the medieval translator of the Latin Vulgate Bible, switches between translating *pomarium* as 'orcherdis' and the rather pleasant-sounding 'appil gardynes'. 'Apple garden' is perhaps a more accurate description of such a place: a garden that happens to have apples growing in it. Apple gardens could be found in monasteries from Llanthony (Gwent) in the west to Norwich (Norfolk) in the east; from Rimpton (Somerset) in the

ABOVE: *The ravishing orchard at Acorn Bank,*
Cumbria, where ancient varieties of apple are grown.

south to Hexham (Northumberland) in the north. The citizens of London laid out 'beautiful and spacious' orchards outside the city walls, and the king himself had one of 8 acres (3.2 hectares) or so beside Windsor Castle, joining the deer park and the pleasure gardens.

In the early sixteenth century the Duke of Buckingham created a walled orchard beside his luxurious new house at Thornbury in Wiltshire, 'full of young grafftes, well laden with frute, many rooses, and other pleasures; and in the same orchard ar many goodley allyes to walk ynne openly'. The 'many rooses', 'pleasures' and 'goodley allyes' show how important orchards were for recreation. Thornbury must have been an enchanting place because not long after

Buckingham finished it, Henry VIII had him executed and took the house for himself. It can still be visited, though the orchard has long gone. John Leland's *Itinerary*, from the same period, mentions another such aristocratic garden at Wressle Castle in Yorkshire. The orchard there had a mount 'writhen about in degrees like turnings of cokilshells to come to the top without payne' – what we would call a 'snail mount' (a mound of earth with a spiral path to the summit). These orchards were at the heart of the grandest ornamental gardens.

The Elizabethans were justly proud of their orchards. The historian William Harrison, writing a decade or so after Elizabeth came to the throne, claimed that English orchards 'were never furnished with so good fruit nor with such variety as at this present'. It was a genuinely exciting time: 'beside that we have most delicate apples, plums, pears, walnuts, filberts, etc., and those of sundry sorts,' wrote Harrison, 'so have we no less store of strange fruit, as apricots, almonds, peaches, figs, corn-trees in noblemen's orchards. I have seen capers, oranges, and lemons, and heard of wild olives growing here, beside other strange trees . . . whose names I know not.'

English gardeners learnt from their foreign counterparts, not only introducing new fruits, but better ways of growing them: training fruit trees on walls was thought to be a great novelty in 1600. Something of the Elizabethan sense of the aesthetic value of orchards can be understood by visiting the restored orchard at Lyveden New Bield in Northamptonshire, which was first laid out by the imprisoned Catholic and architectural connoisseur Sir Thomas Tresham as part of an elaborately symbolic landscape in the late sixteenth century. One of the great early English gardening books, William Lawson's *A New Orchard and Garden* (1618), is a testament to the Elizabethan love of orchards. Lawson wrote from long years of experience – and affection: the orchard, he says, 'takes away the tediousnesse and heavie load of three or four score years'. Typically, he emphasizes both the profit and the sheer pleasure of orchards, which he recommended his readers to embellish with all kinds of ornaments, including the mounts of their aristocratic forbears: 'Mounts of stone or wood, curiously wrought within and without, or of earth covered with fruit trees…with staires of precious workmanship; and in some corner (or moe) a true diall or clock, and some Antickworks and especially silver-sounding Musick, mixt instruments, and voyces, gracing all the rest'. He also recommended that his readers have 'the roots of your trees powdred with Strawberries' – an enchanting idea, but not a new one, as medieval gardeners did the same. Here is something approaching the complete garden: profitable and delightful, offering food, repose and recreation.

✱

Lawson marks the high point of the orchard's place in the English garden. Cromwell's Commonwealth did bring new advances in horticultural science, a topic of keen interest. The influential gardening writer John Rea (d.1681) not only proved how yields could be significantly increased, but recommended that gardeners be forced by law to plant orchards. In the later seventeenth century, however, the tide of fashion seems to have turned. Perhaps the restoration of Charles II brought a reaction by returning Cavaliers against utilitarian Puritans. Certainly, fruit trees could not be clipped in the modishly geometric French style, as lime and hornbeam might be. The eighteenth-century landscape garden, with its abhorrence of walled enclosures, banished orchards to workaday obscurity, and their exclusion from the ornamental garden has largely persisted to this day. Some of the most enchanting Victorian orchards, such as that at Oxburgh Hall, are fascinating attempts to re-create the privileged place reserved for fruit trees in the Tudor garden. Today, however, when conservationists talk of 'historic orchards', they generally mean small-scale commercial orchards, such as those that once occupied so much of Kent, the southwest and the Welsh borders – well worth visiting, but very different from the garden orchards of William Lawson.

PHYSIC GARDENS

THE TERM 'PHYSIC GARDEN' dates from the seventeenth century and describes gardens where plants are grown for scientific but particularly for medicinal, purposes. The word 'physic' itself originally meant the 'study of the human body', but soon came to mean simply 'medicine', hence 'physician'. In fact, 'Phisitions Garden' was the name initially given to the first-ever such garden in England. When it opened at Oxford in 1621, it was renamed the Physic Garden, before its final (and present-day) incarnation as the University of Oxford Botanic Garden.

Of course, there were medicinal gardens long before 1621. The oldest medical books in English – the Anglo-Saxon 'Leech Books' – describe the use of herbs, but it is likely that these were gathered in the wild rather than cultivated. The earliest medicinal gardens were established within the secure confines of monasteries. An idealized Benedictine monastery plan from St Gall (*c.* 816–20) shows an infirmary garden with beds in a *herbarium* for twenty-eight plants, including kidney beans, irises and lilies. The garden probably also included a resting place for patients. As medical knowledge grew, so did the number and variety of

✳

medicinal plants. By the time of the late Middle Ages, a monastic *herbarium* might grow 100 different varieties. These gardens were an invaluable medical resource, and Henry VIII's Dissolution of the Monasteries in the 1530s was a devastating blow.

The first physic garden in Europe was established at the University of Pisa in 1543. It was called a *hortus medicus* (medical garden), though English visitors knew it as the 'Physiq Garden'. Similar gardens followed at Padua in 1545, and at Heidelberg in 1593. Florence established a *giardino dei simplice* (garden of simples) in 1550. A 'simple' was a medicine that consisted of only one 'element', and Renaissance doctors thought that herbs were the obvious example of this. ('Simplers' was the name given to people who gathered herbs for the London apothecary shops.) Medicinal gardens in England remained smaller, private affairs. One of the best known was 'a Physicke Garden or Garden of Simples' cultivated in Long Acre, near Covent Garden in London, by John Parkinson, an accomplished herbalist and apothecary who counted King James among his clients.

Oxford University's Physic Garden was founded on a grand scale by Lord Danvers, but so much money was spent building the impressive walls that none was left for plants. The first keepers of the garden were a father and son both named Jacob Bobart. They were competent herbalists, and men of considerable eccentricity, sometimes more memorable than the plants they cared for. An early visitor recalled: 'We entered the Hortus Medicus and Professor Bobart was waiting for us. I was greatly shocked by the hideous features and villainous appearance of this good and honest man. His wife, a filthy old hag, was with him, and although she may be the ugliest of her sex he is certainly the more repulsive of the two.' The original layout of the garden has been lost, but a late seventeenth-century engraving shows a severely geometric garden, with precise divisions for teaching purposes.

Oxford is one of only two original physic gardens still visible in England; the other is the Chelsea Physic Garden, founded in 1673. (Edinburgh's Royal Botanic Garden was founded as a Physic Garden in 1670, but abandoned its original site in the late eighteenth century.) The Chelsea garden was carved out from land already used by many seventeenth-century market gardeners beside the Thames; the market gardens have all been built over, and only the apothecaries' one survives. The riverside location was particularly useful as a base for herb-gathering expeditions down the river to rural Putney or Battersea. The range of plants used and cultivated by apothecaries expanded significantly in the seventeenth century. Nicholas Culpeper

PHYSIC HERBS IN A GARDEN OF THE 1670s

Angelica	Great valerian	Rhubarb
Asarabacca	Greek valerian	Rue
Bears-foot [Hellebore]	Harts tongue	Scordium
Carduus [Thistle]	Horse raddish	Scorsonera
Dittander	Lavender cotton	Scurvy-grass
Dragons	Liquorish	Smalage
Elecampane	Liverwort	Sneese-wort
Fetherfew	Marshmallows	Solomon's seal
Germander	Master-wort	Southern-wood
Garlick	Mother-wort	Winter cherries
Goats rue	Pelletary of the wall	Wormwood
	Pionies	

listed 358 in his famous *Herball* of 1652, and he concentrated on just the English ones, believing that English diseases needed English cures. One advantage of Culpepper's approach was that physic herbs could be grown or gathered by ordinary people, rather than buying expensive imports from the apothecaries. John Parkinson had advised his readers to cultivate a separate physic garden alongside the kitchen garden, orchard and garden of pleasure, and by the end of the seventeenth century it seems these discrete garden areas were quite common. In his book *The English Gardener*, first published in 1670 and often reprinted thereafter, Leonard Meager compiled a list of thirty-four 'physick herbs' for the ordinary household to cultivate (see above). Visitors to the physic gardens at Chelsea and Oxford, however, were chiefly attracted by the novel exotics grown there. Celia Fiennes, who visited Oxford in the 1680s, was one such example. 'The Physick garden,' she wrote, 'afforded great diversion and pleasure, the variety of flowers and plants would have entertained one a week.' Among the 'remarkable things' she saw was 'the sensible plant, take but a Leafe between finger and thumb and squeeze it and it immediately Curles up together as if pained and after some tyme opens abroad again… There

❀

is also the humble plant that grows on a long slender Stalke and do but strike it, it falls flatt on the ground stalke and all, and after some tyme revives againe and Stands up.'

Gradually, the botanic role of the gardens was taking over: the Chelsea garden became known as 'the Botanic Gardens, Chelsea' throughout the eighteenth century, and Oxford's was similarly renamed in 1840. The gardens still had a medical function: Chelsea was an early source for the anti-malarial drug quinine, obtained from the bark of the cinchona tree, and important at a time when malaria was still common in marshland areas of Britain. But these gardens were simply too small to provide medicinal plants on the necessary scale; a seventeenth-century bill for 150 lb (68 kg) of mint to be distilled for oil shows the quantities required. The Chelsea garden was used for teaching Victorian medical students, but in 1895 the study of herbs was removed from the medical syllabus, and three years later the Society of Apothecaries gave up its 300-year ownership of the garden. Ironically, it was only in 1898, when the Chelsea garden was taken over by a charitable trust, that it acquired the new, anachronistic name that remains to the present day: the Chelsea Physic Garden.

▣ SLIPS

ALSO KNOWN AS 'SLIP GARDENS', slips are strips of land immediately outside the kitchen garden. Sometimes these areas are used as nurseries, and it might be no coincidence that the cut shoot of a plant used for propagation is also called a slip. It is more likely, however, that the name reflects the old use of 'slip' – a narrow strip of land. The oldest example that we have come across dates from Jacobean times, but slip gardens really became common from the mid-eighteenth century – possibly because the range of vegetables had increased, and there was no longer room to grow everything within the walled garden. Something had to move outside, and the choice naturally fell on the hardier plants – what Mrs Beeton called the 'coarse vegetables' – artichokes, rhubarb, horseradish. Fruit bushes are often grown in slips, as are some orchard trees: the external walls of the kitchen garden are ideal for training fruit trees. The malodorous compost yards and melon grounds were often also confined to the slips. A slip garden might be up to 50 feet (15 m) deep, and as long as the garden to which they are joined; the most favoured site for ripening fruit would be the warmer, south-facing external walls, but you will find slips on every side of a kitchen garden, depending on the space available.

Vineyards

VINEYARDS HAVE BEEN planted in England since the third century AD. In the year 278 the Emperor Probus issued a decree encouraging viticulture throughout the Roman Empire. It wasn't a terribly good idea as far as he personally was concerned, for when he ordered his soldiers to give up their free time in order to cultivate vines, they promptly mutinied and killed him. But on the ground in England there were more positive results, with vineyards being planted at least as far north as Lincolnshire. The latitude is important because vines, of course, require warmth to flourish, and this has not always been reliably available. Average temperatures in England started rising round about the year 1000, reached a peak in the late thirteenth century, and began to decline from around 1400. The coldest period in modern times stretched roughly from 1550 to 1700, with temperatures rising from around 1800, and accelerating notably in the last decade of the twentieth century. Wine-makers in England now enjoy their most auspicious climate for many centuries.

It is unlikely that the Anglo-Roman vineyards survived the fall of the empire, but the Venerable Bede mentions vineyards in the eighth century, and these may have been descendants of those originals. Under King Alfred, in the late ninth century, they were in fact protected by law, which indicates their importance. The eleventh-century Domesday Book records no fewer than thirty-eight vineyards in England, all of them in southern counties, and including a newly planted one of 4 acres (1.6 hectares) at Westminster. This southern concentration may be a reflection not so much of climate, as of the fact that the vine-nurturing monasteries in the north had almost all been sacked by Vikings over the previous century. Under the stability of the new regime, and with a warmer climate, viticulture flourished in the late Middle Ages. Ely in Cambridgeshire, for example, was well known for its wines: the Normans called it 'Ile des Vignes'. The Bishop of Ely also had a vineyard at his house in London – whence the name Vine Street. King Edward IV had a 'vineyard of pleasure' at Windsor, which foreign dignitaries visited during the fifteenth century. The vine was also one of the most important medieval garden plants: it was the most popular climber and, when grown over arbours and other supports, the chief source of shade in the garden.

In Elizabethan gardens, by way of contrast, vines were surprisingly scarce: William Harrison writes in 1577 of the 'long discontinuance' of vine growing, and observes that the plant is rarely cultivated 'for pleasure and shadow' (i.e. in a garden), let alone in entire fields or vineyards. The decline was due partly to Henry VIII's destruction of the monasteries, which owned over a third of the country's vineyards; partly to the worsening weather; and partly to the availability of cheap wine imported from the Continent. This did at least give the vine a certain cachet, as a kind of expensive curiosity. When the Lord Chancellor Robert Cecil built his extravagant house at Hatfield in the early seventeenth century, he had 20,000 vines sent over by the wife of the French ambassador. Hatfield's vineyard became as much of a tourist attraction as the extraordinary house: John Evelyn, visiting thirty years later, remarked that 'the most considerable rarity besides the house…was the Garden & Vineyard rarely [unusually] well water'd and planted'. Outside Hatfield, vineyards were few and far between. King James had them, of course, including a small 'vine garden' at Westminster, and another at Oatlands in Surrey, a place reserved for the 'planting of new and rare fruits, flowers, herbs and trees'. But when Samuel Pepys saw a vineyard by chance in 1665 it was, he confessed, 'the first that ever I did see'.

In the early eighteenth century the plantsmen London and Wise were supplying twenty-three different kinds of vine from their Brompton Park Nursery, which shows that interest among the seriously wealthy had perhaps increased. Interestingly, vineyards were briefly favoured by the most advanced landscape gardeners of the time. The writer Alexander Pope planted one in his celebrated garden at Twickenham, while John Pitt, the surveyor general for woods and forests, established a small ornamental vineyard at the centre of the pastoral landscape at Encombe in Dorset. Another ornamental vineyard was planted by Charles Hamilton on a spectacular lakeside location at Painshill in Surrey around 1740. This one has recently been restored, and can be visited today to experience a moment when, for the first time since the Middle Ages, vines became once more a significant part of the pleasure garden.

In 1768 the so-called 'Great Vine' was planted at Hampton Court, probably by Capability Brown. It was not part of a landscape garden, but grown in a glasshouse devoted to exotic plants – or rather, grown with its branches inside the glasshouse and its roots in the soil outside, as was common practice. Growing vines under glass for their grapes was the commonest garden use of them in the nineteenth century – although Lord Bute, another wealthy enthusiast, planted 3 acres (1.2 hectares) beside Castle Coch, his wonderful fake medieval pile in South Glamorgan, still flourishing today. In the warming climate enjoyed by present-day gardens the vine is most commonly found trained across a pergola, for example: a medieval shade plant once again coming into its own.

CHAPTER FIVE

WATER

Dear water, clear water, playful in all your streams,
As you dash or loiter through life who does not love
To sit beside you, to hear you and see you,
Pure being, perfect in music and movement?
'STREAMS', W.H. AUDEN

THERE IS A FASCINATING, contradictory quality about water's place in our gardens. On the one hand it is assuredly, as Auden wrote, a 'pure being': one of the four ancient elements believed to constitute all life, possessed of an abiding, mystical attraction for humans. On the other hand, its presence in the garden has always been dependent on hard-headed advances in technology: from the Egyptian *shaduf* (irrigation bucket), through Greek and later Arab developments of the science of hydraulics, to intricately engineered Victorian fountains, and the elaborate water features in aluminium and glass favoured by contemporary garden designers. Besides all this, water is, of course, essential to the life and growth of our plants. We can grow our gardens without soil or sunlight, but water is the one thing that we have not learnt to dispense with. No other garden element is at the same time so basic in need, so complex in manipulation, and so indefinable in attraction.

Water offers all kinds of gifts to the garden besides that fundamental one of life. In fountains, waterfalls, streams and cascades it provides motion, a dramatic contrast to the quieter, more subdued movement of branches and leaves. In canals and ponds it offers stillness and repose. Laid out in strong, linear forms, it provides order and structure;

LEFT: *Alders growing beside the medieval lake at Lakeside, Whitbourne. Alders are invaluable for water-side planting, as they will tolerate a soaking that would rot many other trees.*

BELOW: *Formal waterways played an important
part in ancient gardens, including this example
from Egypt.*

alternatively, in the sinuous lines of streams, rills and gently curving banks of a lake it can soften the geometry of a too sternly structured garden. Its sound is infinitely diverting; its coolness tempers the heat of the sun; its reflective qualities embellish and amplify long views.

Water features in the English garden are not quite so universally prevalent as those on the continent of Europe. This is partly a matter of climate, and partly of topography. England's moderate temperatures mean that gardeners and garden-owners have never felt that urgent need for the cooling presence of water in the landscape – unlike the French, Spanish and Italians; nor have English gardens benefited from the traditions that grow out of that need – the wonderful water gardens of the Alhambra in Spain, for example. In terms of topography, English landowners in general have not favoured the steep hillside locations that characterize the gardens of Moorish Spain, or those of Italian Renaissance villas, with their numerous opportunities for the spectacular flow of water. One of the prime requirements of Italian villas such as the revolutionary Villa Medici at Fiesole (late fifteenth century) was *un' abondanza ghrande d'aqqua* (a great abundance of water) with which you could *fare mille belle chose* (do a thousand beautiful things), as one of the Villa's builders, Giovanni di Luca Rossi, wrote in 1455.

RIGHT: *The Temple of Ancient Virtue at Stowe, Buckinghamshire, designed and landscaped by William Kent in 1737 to be reflected in the still waters of the stream, named the Worthies, flowing below.*

LEFT: A late medieval fountain. Note the spouts point downwards, as hydraulic technology was not sufficiently developed to power them upwards.

Having said that, water has played an important and sometimes central part in English gardens since the time of the Roman occupation. If you visit the Roman villa at Fishbourne in Sussex, you will see the remains of a dozen fountains and basins. We know that other Roman villas featured ornamental ponds, and at least one possessed a fountain house – all, of course, now lost. Some of the greatest water gardens were laid out by Roman emperors, such as Hadrian and Tiberius; and when these were explored and catalogued by eighteenth-century antiquarians they provided inspiration for a new generation of landscape gardeners – of which more anon.

For medieval water gardens there is, as might be expected, a similar dearth of visible, physical evidence. None of the water features we describe below can be seen in their original state, though the remains of ponds, moats and suchlike can still be traced. Medieval illustrations of gardens, however, feature a wealth of fountains, streams and ponds; and in medieval poetry and other texts water seems to be highly valued – more so, for example, than flowers. Chaucer describes a garden fed by 'colde well-streames… That swimmen full of smale fishes light, With finnes red, and scales silver bright'. He goes on to say:

RIGHT: *This woodcut shows the Emperor Maximilian I seated in a garden beside a fountain. It was designed in the early 16th century by Hans Burgkmair for Maxmilian's biography* The White King, *and its elaborate design reflects the emperor's keen interest in the arts.*

I ne can the number tell
Of streames small that by device
…[came] through the condys [conduit, or fountain pipe],
Of which the water, in running,
Gan make a noise full liking…

This sounds like another medieval water feature described by Boccaccio, in which a system of small channels carried water running throughout the entire garden. Chaucer's contemporary John Lydgate (?1370–1449) describes garden streams running over beds of golden gravel – an ornamental embellishment still used in Jacobean times. And the poet Stephen Hawes (c.1475–1511) records a 'respendysshaunt…dulcet spring and marvellous fountain/ Of gold and azure made all certain'.

Fountains seem to have been an important and prestigious element in the medieval garden. Albertus Magnus, writing around 1260, recommends that 'if possible a clear fountain of water in a stone basin should be in the midst, for its purity gives much pleasure'. It should be remembered, however, that until the early seventeenth century the word 'fountain' can refer to any basin of water fed by a pipe, and that the spectacle might consist of water falling into the basin, rather than a jet being thrown up (see page 188).

RIGHT: *Another late medieval fountain, feeding a hexagonal basin typical of the period.*

The two main uses for water in the medieval garden were irrigation, of course, and the keeping of fish – an important food source. Fish-ponds were often linked into series, as we shall see, and these supremely useful garden elements were also exploited for their aesthetic possibilities. The royal gardens at Woodstock in Oxfordshire contained a linked series of ponds, of which the last can still be seen beside Capability Brown's lake. The bishop's palace at Worcester had a garden of 2 acres (0.8 hectares) with not one, but two moats, which in turn fed a sequence of linked fish-ponds below; while Abbot Godfrey of Peterborough made for himself 'four lovely pools' within a walled garden at Eye in Cambridgeshire.

The Renaissance saw one of those crucial technological advances in the use of water. As so often, the advance was not a discovery but a rediscovery – in this case, of the science of hydraulics. Greek scholars had thoroughly explored the possibilities of water flow, and around the time of Christ, Hero of Alexandria wrote his *Pneumatics*, which gave examples of how the passage of water could be used to make statues move, trumpets sound or birds sing. The *Pneumatics* was finally published in Latin in 1501, a millennium and a half after it was first written; and it was the rediscovery of treatises such as this that encouraged the proliferation of fountains and other water devices in European gardens in the sixteenth century. Typically, these were first seen in Italian gardens – the Villa d'Este at Tivoli, for example, had a musical water organ – but both the technology, and reports from astonished visitors, had reached England by the middle of Elizabeth I's reign; and the business of inventive imitation began. The queen herself installed a fountain in the principal garden at Hampton Court around 1590: 'a splendid high and massy fountain, with an ingenious water-work, by which you can, if you like, make the water to play upon

❋

the ladies and others who are standing by, and give them a thorough wetting'. Highly contrived water features were created at many royal and aristocratic gardens during this period. They included Theobalds in Hertfordshire, which had a summer-house surrounded by ponds and ornamented by a water-driven revolving table; and Hatfield, where the bed of the lord chancellor's artificial stream was lined with coloured pebbles and shells, which the gardener John Tradescant had personally fetched from Paris. None of these creations survive, alas, though some idea of the effect of water in the grandest Elizabethan gardens can be glimpsed by visiting the remaining sixteenth-century villa gardens of Italy.

The development of garden hydraulics continued in the seventeenth century, and perhaps the finest examples were to be found at Chatsworth in Derbyshire. In 1700 Dr Charles Leigh published his *Natural History of Lancashire, Cheshire, and the Peak in Derbyshire; with an account of the British, Phonician, Armenian, Greek and Roman antiquities in those Parts.* Among all those antiquities, Dr Leigh helpfully included an account of how Chatsworth looked at the time:

> *The gardens, very delightful, pleasant and stately, adorn'd with exquisite water works; the first we observe is Neptune with his sea nymphs from whence, by the turning of a cock, immediately issue forth several columns of water, which seem'd to fall upon sea-weeds. Not far from this is another pond, where sea-horses continually roll; and near to this stands a tree, composed of copper, which exactly resembles a willow; by the turn of a cock each leaf distils continually drops of water, and lively represents a shower of rain; from this we passed by a grove of cypress, upon an ascent, and came to a cascade, at the top of which stand two sea-nymphs, with each a jar under the arm; the water falling thence upon a cascade, whilst they seem to squeeze the vessels, produces a loud rumbling noise, like what we may imagine of the Egyptian or Indian cataracts. At the bottom of the cascade there is another pond, in which is an artificial rose, by turning of a cock the water ascends through it, and hangs suspended in the air in the figure of that flower. There is another pond, wherein is Mercury pointing at the gods and throwing up water...*

The artificial willow has since been replaced by a Victorian copy, but the cascade is still there – the only original cascade visible in England. The other great seventeenth-century waterworks were those created at Boughton in Northamptonshire, which included a cascade, numerous fountains, and a French-influenced 'water parterre', in which the scrolls and turns of the conventionally patterned parterre were replaced by shaped ponds. Just how water was valued by seventeenth-century gardeners can be gleaned from the following advice given by John Woolridge in 1677:

> *…a Fair stream or Current flowing through or neer your Garden adds much to the Glory of it. On the banks of it may you plant several aquatick Exoticks, & have your seats or places of repose under their Umbrage, and there satiate your self with the view of the Curling Streams and its nimble Inhabitants. These Gliding Streams refrigerate the Air in a Summer evening, and render their banks so pleasant, that they become resistless Charms to your Senses, by the murmuring Noise, the Undulation of the Water, the verdant Banks and Shades over them, the sporting Fish confin'd within your own limits, the beautiful Swans, and by the pleasant notes of singing Birds, that delight in Groves on the Banks of such Rivulets.*

This enthusiasm comes close to a delight in water for its natural state and qualities. In fact, the late seventeenth century marked the high point in the artificial forms of water: the chief influence here was Louis XIV's gardens at Versailles, many of which were created during the 1660s. Versailles was not endowed with great supplies of water, despite being built on marshland (the marsh gases killed hundreds of soldiers forced to excavate the king's lakes): eventually the

'Machine de Marly', a gigantic pumping station, was built on the banks of the Seine to pump water 165 yards (150 m) uphill, where it could begin a 2-mile (3-km) descent to Versailles. There was still insufficient water to fill all 1400 fountains in the grounds, so the *fontainier* Charles Denis had to turn them on in sequence as the king wandered through the gardens.

England could match neither the political nor the spending power of Louis XIV, but the French manipulation of water was important in the gardens created by the restored Charles II and his court from 1660. The canal at St James's Park, created by the French royal gardener André Mollet around 1660, has long disappeared, but the Long Water at Hampton Court, dating from 1666, still survives, as does the later, possibly Dutch-influenced canal at Westbury Court in Gloucestershire.

These formal elements continued to be created into the following century, and there is a wonderful example in the gardens laid out by Thomas Coke at Melbourne Hall, Derbyshire, from 1704. But, as with so many aspects of landscape during that period, the lure of informality was starting to be heeded – at least among the cognoscenti. It seems to have been Bishop Matthew Wren (an uncle of the architect Christopher Wren) who first came up with the revolutionary idea that a piece of water might follow a curving line rather than a straight one. Wren spent eighteen years without trial in the Tower of London after falling foul of radical Protestants, before being released in time for Charles II's restoration. He had much time on his hands, and besides rewriting the Book of Common Prayer, he studied architecture and gardening, noting: 'For disposing the current of a river to a mighty length in a little space, I invented the serpentine, a form admirably conveying the current in circles and yet contrary motions upon one and the same level, with walks and retirements between, to the advantage of all purposes, either of gardenings, plantings, or banquetings, or aery delights'.

Wren's idea did not find practical form until the beginning of the eighteenth century, when Lord Bathurst claimed to have created the first-ever 'winding stream' in a garden. It was so unprecedented that a visiting friend thought the only possible reason for it was to save money, and mocked Bathurst for not spending a little more on a straight canal. By 1730 even Queen Caroline was at it, creating the Serpentine lake in Hyde Park. William Kent's layout at Rousham, Oxfordshire, is the great example of the informal and serpentine use of water in the period, and within a decade, the informal style had become the fashionable norm. The scholar and man of letters Joseph Spence (1699–1768) advised that 'if your ground be all dry,

CHAPTER FIVE:
WATER

LEFT: *The Temple of Piety at Studley
Royal, Yorkshire, overlooks the curving
lines of the Moon Pond.*

a winding stream should be brought into it, if possible; if not, pieces of water, with alders and weeping willows and other aquatics about them, dashed here and there'. Meanwhile, the journalist John Shebbeare remarked in 1755 that 'the *jet d'eau* is quite out of fashion in this kingdom; the cascade, and falling streams bubbling amongst rocks, the winding river without regularity of figure, or strait parallel lines, make the water-works of this country'. In the late 1740s Capability Brown created his first-ever lake on the Duke of Grafton's estate at Wakefield Lodge in Northamptonshire, and from then on he was unstoppable. Brown is sometimes disparaged for the destruction of earlier gardens that his new layouts entailed, and for the apparent monotony of his style. But in his manipulation of water he came close to genius. His most famous lake is that at Blenheim in Oxfordshire (see page 193), but perhaps the most artful is at Wootton in the same county.

The technological advances of the nineteenth century brought a new impetus to the more spectacular water features – especially fountains. Perhaps the most significant use of water in the period is to be seen in Joseph Paxton's gardens at Chatsworth, and in William Nesfield's at Witley Court. Typically Victorian, they are showy to the point of vulgarity, and technically brilliant. We look at both in the section on fountains (see pages 188–90), but it is perhaps fair to say that water gardens did not occupy first place on the Victorian gardener's wishlist.

The eclecticism of the twentieth century is hard to summarize in a few lines, though it is certainly true that the formal, architectural use of water made a brilliant comeback. Edwin Lutyens, Harold Peto and Geoffrey Jellicoe all made outstanding contributions to that tradition in the gardens at Hestercombe in Somerset, Buscot Park in Oxfordshire, and Shute House in Dorset – whilst, closer to the present day, even the *giochi d'acqua* (literally 'water jokes') have returned, in the form of the mischievous water maze of Hever Castle in Kent. More details of gardens that can be visited today can be found in the rest of this chapter and on pages 262–7.

▦ BASINS

A BASIN (SOMETIMES spelt 'bason') can take one of two different forms. The more general form is the bowl or small pool at the base of a fountain or cascade. The more specific form is a geometrical pond, usually stone-lined, which can be circular, square, hexagonal or octagonal. This form is peculiar to the formal gardens of the seventeenth and eighteenth centuries, and many basins of the period have vanished under new developments of later periods. Three such examples are the Round Basin excavated by Charles Bridgeman at Claremont in Surrey, which later became a more 'natural' lake; the Great Basin at Stowe in Buckinghamshire; and the 215-foot (65-m) octagonal basin created at Boughton in Northamptonshire in around 1720. The late seventeenth-century traveller Celia Fiennes records many 'basons' in her visits to country houses; for her the word seems to have denoted almost any ornamental, artificially constructed pond. One example that still survives is the octagonal basin in the central avenue at Wimpole House, Cambridgeshire.

CANALS

THE CANAL IS ONE of the garden elements that we owe to the Restoration of Charles II (1660). An early (and not very effective) industrial canal had been cut at Exeter in 1566, but the first ornamental canal – at least in Europe – was excavated at Fleury-en-Bière in France in the late sixteenth century. French canal building took a great leap forward with the career of André Le Notre, who created the canals at Vaux-le-Vicomte in the 1650s and those at Versailles in the 1660s. It was these monumental French canals that were re-created (on a slightly less grandiose scale) by the returning Charles II. The first was in St James's Park, and was designed by André Mollet. Charles had asked for the services of Le Notre, but Louis XIV needed him in France and sent Mollet instead, the son of Le Notre's former master. The diarist Samuel Pepys watched the St James's canal being cut in September 1660, little more than three months after Charles's arrival in London. This was quickly followed by the Long Water or Long Canal at Hampton Court, which was all but finished by 1662. Unlike St James's, this canal can still be visited.

The canal was an important feature of the very formal, geometric gardens laid out towards the end of the seventeenth century and into the first years of the following one. Other examples were created at Westbury Court, near the banks of the Severn in Gloucestershire, in 1695 – this one looking a little more Dutch in inspiration, following the accession of a Dutch royal family – and at Wrest Park in Bedfordshire, in 1711 – another Long Water. Few of these geometric waterways were excavated after the first decades of the eighteenth century, and the St James's Park canal was changed into an informal lake in the early nineteenth century. A limited revival can, however, be seen in the twentieth, as at Harold Peto's Buscot Park in Oxfordshire.

CASCADES

CASCADES WERE FIRST CREATED in Italian gardens in the early seventeenth century: the English word comes from the French, *cascade*, which inherits the Italian *cascata*, or 'fall'. The cascade at the Villa Aldobrandini, near Rome, was made around 1600, and seen forty-five years later by John Evelyn, who was travelling to escape the Civil Wars in England. Evelyn's description is worth quoting in full because it shows just how impressive Italian gardens could be for English visitors, particularly in their use of water.

> *Just behind the palace (which is of excellent architecture) in the centre of the inclosure, rises a high hill, or mountain, all over clad with tall wood, and so formed by nature, as if it had been cut out by art, from the summit whereof falls a cascade, seeming rather a great river than a stream precipitating into a large theatre of water, representing an exact and perfect rainbow, when the sun shines out. Under this, is made an artificial grot, wherein are curious rocks, hydraulic organs, and all sorts of singing birds, moving and chirping by force of the water, with several other pageants and surprising inventions. In the centre of one of these rooms, rises a copper ball that continually dances about three feet above the pavement, by virtue of a wind conveyed secretly to a hole beneath it; with many other devices to wet the unwary spectators, so that one can hardly step without wetting to the skin. In one of these theaters of water, is an Atlas spouting up the stream to a very great height; and another monster makes a terrible roaring with a horn; but, above all, the representation of a storm is most natural, with such fury of rain, wind, and thunder, as one would imagine oneself in some extreme tempest.*

Evelyn built himself a little cascade at his brother's house in Wootton in Oxfordshire; but the earliest surviving English cascade – indeed, the only survival from the seventeenth century – is at Chatsworth. Created in 1696, it was restored in 1994–6, and children (or adults for that matter) can still happily splash on its steps. Another, vast cascade was built almost concurrently at Dyrham Park in Gloucestershire. Like so many others, the gardens at Dyrham

were smoothed out in the eighteenth century, and much of the earlier garden lost, but the form of the cascade can still be traced. More 'naturalistic' cascades were created at some eighteenth-century estates, notably at Bowood in Wiltshire and at Blenheim in Oxfordshire, both beautiful examples created by Capability Brown (though the former was designed by Charles Hamilton, who was also responsible for Painshill in Surrey). During the nineteenth century, Chatsworth's ingenious head gardener Joseph Paxton created a new cascade, a typically

Left: *The cascade at Groombridge Place, Kent, which feeds the Blue Pool below. Within the cascade a statue of Neptune holds a shell from which the water flows.*

CHAPTER FIVE:
WATER

❀

audacious construction of enormous boulders. By this date it is difficult to tell apart the 'naturalistic' cascade from the waterfall (see pages 200–1). A return to the more formal origins of the cascade can be seen today in many public parks and water sculptures.

▦ COLD BATHS

A COLD BATH IS TYPICALLY, though not always, found in eighteenth-century gardens. It was, as its name suggests, simply a bath of cold water – sometimes in the open air, sometimes incorporated into a building (see Chapter Six). Cold baths were created by the Romans, and can still be seen in the remains of Pompeii; in fact, the Roman example probably inspired eighteenth-century architects and gardeners, who prided themselves on their 'Augustan' inheritance. Cold baths were often located on the site of springs, which guaranteed low temperatures for the water. They were supposed to provide medical benefits, though not everyone was convinced of their efficacy. In a satirical essay in the *Tatler* of 1710, Richard Steele takes on the character of a doctor treating a patient, whom he concludes 'was far gone in the spleen'. Spleen was thought to be one of the hot 'humours' of the body: 'I therefore advised him to rise the next morning and plunge into the cold bath, there to remain under water until he was almost drowned. This I ordered him to repeat six days successively…'

The earliest example of a cold bath was probably found at Theobalds in the late sixteenth century, but most date from at least a century later. Rousham possesses an open-air cold bath designed by William Kent around 1738, and fed by the rill mentioned on page 200. The Duke of Newcastle's grotto at Oaklands Park in Surrey, built almost contemporaneously, contained a cold bath with water 'as clear as crystal and as cold as ice'. The cold bath at Stowe (now lost) was constructed to offer bathers not only cold water, but outstanding views, as described by the novelist Samuel Richardson (1689–1761): '…we came to the Cold-bath, from whence we beheld a natural Cascade falling down from the Octagon, in Three different Sheets of Water, into a large Lake. One of the Sheets glides thro' an Arch, or Piece of Ruin, which is mostly hid by a Clump of Evergreens; but his Lordship, as we are told, designs to make a good deal of Amendment to it, tho' at present it has a very natural and agreeable Appearance.' The hardy Victorians continued to build cold baths in their gardens, but the fashion was never quite as popular as it had been in the previous century.

FOUNTAINS

'FOUNTAINES I INTEND to be of two Natures: the One that sprinckleth or Spouteth Water; the Other a Faire Receipt of Water…without Fish, or Slime, or Mud.' As Francis Bacon points out, the word 'fountain' originally denoted two slightly different water features. The earlier and simpler form was that of a basin fed by a pipe or spring (see pages 182–3). Shakespeare alludes to this one in the words he gives the hapless Achilles: 'my mind is troubled, like a fountain stirred, And I myself see not the

ABOVE: *An early medieval fountain and basin set within a walled garden.*

bottom of it.' By Shakespeare and Bacon's time, however, a new form was in use – the now-familiar spouting fountain – and it is this form that has come to dominate. That new form was a consequence of the rediscovered science of hydraulics, which in the sixteenth century spread from Italy to France, and to England by around 1590: one of the earliest substantial fountains in England was installed in that year by Elizabeth I at Hampton Court. Sometimes the spouting fountain is known by the French name, *jet d'eau*; sometimes by another corruption, *jetteau*, which combines the French name with the Italian for 'jet', *getto*; and sometimes by the anglicized version of the Italian word *jetto*. All three names give us clues as to how fountain technology reached us.

Fountains of water…shall be embellished with plants and buildings.
PLATO

The fall of water is Nature's province – only the vulgar citizen…squirts up his rivulets in jettaux.
WILLIAM SHENSTONE

The great age of the fountain in the English garden is indeed the late sixteenth and early seventeenth centuries, when these startling new devices were considered wonders of human invention, a prerequisite for (and only affordable in) the grandest royal and aristocratic gardens. Unfortunately, none of these early creations have survived – though fountains, as we shall see, have enjoyed later moments of renaissance. Queen Elizabeth's fountains at Hampton Court in Surrey were celebrated, as were those in the gardens at Nonsuch in Surrey, redeveloped in Elizabeth's honour by Lord Lumley:

> *In the pleasure and artificial gardens are many columns and pyramids of marble, two fountains that spurt water one round the other like a pyramid, upon which are perched small birds that stream water out of their bills. In the Grove of Diana is a very agreeable fountain with Actaeon turned into a stag, as he was sprinkled by the goddess and her nymphs, with inscriptions. There is besides another pyramid of marble full of concealed pipes, which spurt upon all that come within their reach.*

This last device is a *giochi d'acqua*, about which there is more below. The material of choice for fountains was white marble. Nonsuch possessed at least two: one included a statue of a pelican (an important emblem for Elizabethans), which was believed to peck its own breast to provide blood for its young to feed on – a symbol of the queen giving her life for her subjects. There were also large white marble fountains at Hatfield and Theobalds in

Hertfordshire, Wilton in Wiltshire, Kenilworth in Warwickshire, and Wimbledon – all now vanished.

As hydraulic technology became more widely available, fountains became a familiar part of the more restrained geometric parterres of seventeenth-century gardens – though not quite the elaborate centrepieces they had been in Elizabeth's time. During the eighteenth century they tended to become less popular – William Shenstone's censures, quoted at the beginning of this section, are an extreme example of this. More recently, garden fountains have found new popularity in the nineteenth and late twentieth centuries – in both cases as a result of new technology. The inventive Joseph Paxton, who created the Crystal Palace, also erected what was until recently the highest garden fountain in England, at Chatsworth, in 1843. Paxton had to excavate a new 8-acre (3-hectare) reservoir, the Emperor Lake, to feed the fountain – on a hillside 2½ miles (4 km) away, with 220 tons of pipework linking the two. The Emperor Fountain was only recently surpassed in height by the Great Fountain at Stanway House, near Cheltenham in Gloucestershire; which reminds us that the widespread availability of relatively sophisticated hydraulic technology has meant that fountains today can be found in any and every domestic garden; while in public spaces – for example, the Fountain Court at Somerset House, London – they can be programmed by computer to run through intricate sequences, lit by dazzling fibre-optics.

GIOCHI D'ACQUA

TAKING THEIR NAME from an Italian phrase that means 'water games' *giochi d'acqua*, like cascades (and so many other water features), originate in the gardens of Renaissance Italy. These gardens featured 'joke' fountains that could be triggered to play on unsuspecting visitors; and, perhaps more impressive, they also included automata powered by hydraulic pressure. Originally

LEFT: *Fountain statues within the gardens at Heidelberg Castle, near Stuttgart, Germany, probably designed by Salomon de Caus in the early years of the 17th century.*

CHAPTER FIVE:
WATER

❋

distinct, both types of device have come to be called *giochi d'acqua*, and we follow that convention.

Perhaps the first large-scale collection of *giochi d'acqua* was assembled at the Villa d'Este, near Rome, in the late sixteenth century. Although they were visited by English tourists, the best description of them, including their famous water-driven organ, comes from the French philosopher Michel de Montaigne in 1580:

> *The music of the organ, which is real music and a natural organ, though always playing the same thing, is effected by means of the water, which falls with great violence into a round arched cave and agitates the air that is in there and forces it, in order to get out, to go through the pipes of the organ and supply it with wind. Another stream of water, driving a wheel with certain teeth on it, causes the organ keyboard to be struck in a certain order; so you hear an imitation of the sound of trumpets. In another place you hear the song of birds, which are little bronze flutes that you see at regals [on organs]; they give a sound like those little earthenware pots full of water that little children blow into by the spout, this by an artifice like that of the organ; and then by other springs they set in motion an owl, which, appearing at the top of the rock, makes this harmony cease instantly, for the birds are frightened by his presence; and then he leaves the place to them again.*

Montaigne also delighted in the *giochi d'acqua* at the Villa Medici in Castello (near Florence), which showered visitors to its grotto. These devices became something of a craze in aristocratic gardens in Europe. Although few remain in Italy, some can still be experienced at Hellbrunn in Austria, including a table at which nine of the ten seats spout water on the diners – the tenth being reserved, of course, for the dry host. They had reached England by around 1575, when Lord Lumley installed them in the gardens at Nonsuch. A particularly elaborate and celebrated collection was assembled by Thomas Bushell, the 'Wizard of Enstone' – a former servant of Francis Bacon, who launched his own career as a magus after his master's death. But no early *giochi d'acqua* survive in England. Chatsworth in the late seventeenth century had an artificial willow tree that showered visitors to the garden, which was replaced by a nineteenth-century re-creation that is still performing its job admirably. The form might yet, however, enjoy a comeback. Recently at Hever Castle in Kent a water maze has been created in which visitors trying to reach the centre trigger jets of water aimed directly at them: it has proved almost as popular with adults as with children.

LAKES

THE WORD 'LAKE' is French in origin, only commonly used in English from the fourteenth century. Within our gardens, lakes came to prominence in the eighteenth century, though in many landscapes of the period a lake will be called a 'piece of water', or even more simply a 'pond'. They were first created by devotees of the Arcadian ideals of the early 1700s, who were in turn inspired by (amongst other things) the paintings of Claude Lorrain. These often featured idyllic waterside landscapes, and they announced the aesthetic possibilities of large sheets of water within the countryside. One of the earliest was made at Cirencester Park in Gloucestershire by Stephen Switzer and owner Lord Bathurst. Like so many lakes that followed, it was carefully landscaped so that you couldn't quite tell where it ended – an important principle for eighteenth-century lake-makers. One of the many paradoxes of gardeners of the period is that in their dislike for the artificiality and confinement of the old geometric gardens, they were forced to disguise the confines of their lakes artificially to make the landscape appear more open. As Alexander Pope remarked, 'He gains all who pleasingly confounds,/ Surprises, varies and conceals the bounds'.

Another example of the technique is the beautiful lake at Painshill in Surrey, created by Charles Hamilton in the 1740s, which appears to flow on into the countryside beyond Walton Bridge, when it fact it stops right there. Possibly the greatest lake landscape of the eighteenth century is that laid out at Stourhead in Wiltshire by several generations of the Hoare family. Henry Hoare II created it around 1754, then ornamented it with a series of temples and other buildings to provide the visitor with a sequence of extraordinary views. Horace Walpole described it in 1762 as 'one of the most picturesque scenes in the world', and few today would disagree.

The great master of lake creation in the eighteenth century was, of course, Capability Brown. Amongst the many examples of his work are the lakes at Bowood in Wiltshire, Petworth in Sussex and Blenheim in Oxfordshire. All three wonderfully illustrate Brown's ability to disguise the true extent of a piece of water. The lake at Petworth, for example, is serpentine in shape: the ends curl away out of sight, and their shores are thickly planted to conceal the point at which they terminate. At Blenheim, Brown inherited an estate already subject to considerable landscaping and ornamentation by Charles Bridgeman, John Vanbrugh and James Hawksmoor. Brown's masterstroke was to flood the valley in front of the house, where the river was dominated by Vanbrugh's monumental bridge: an extraordinary piece of architecture, but clearly out of scale with the wider landscape. The bottom half of the bridge was submerged by the new lake to create a new and perfectly proportioned feature: the dam Brown built was out of sight of the bridge itself, and few of his drawings have survived, so how he arrived at the correct water level without the aid of modern surveying instruments remains a mystery. The waterworks within the dam still operate today, nearly two and half centuries later.

Not all Brown's work was so happily achieved, however. At Milton Abbas in Dorset, the Earl of Dorchester wished to move a local village to make way for new landscaping; the villagers didn't want to go, but Brown flooded the valley and their houses with his lake anyway. He designed a new village for them nearby, which, ironically, is visited today as an example of the perfect eighteenth-century settlement. Similar objections have ensured that few ornamental lakes have been created since the eighteenth century, though the great Victorian public parks offer some exceptions, such as the lake at Birkenhead, Merseyside (1843).

MOATS

THE EARLIEST WATER-FILLED moats were probably built by the Romans – there are examples at Chester in Cheshire and Towcester in Northamptonshire – but the word itself is a gift of the Normans, and most of our surviving moats are medieval. In origin, of course, the moat was a means of defence, but its aesthetic possibilities were realized very early on. By the end of the thirteenth century, for example, the Bishop of Worcester had built a double-moated garden of 2 acres (0.8 hectares) at his palace; and in 1302 Abbot Godfrey of Peterborough built a 'beautiful herber', which also possessed double moats. Unfortunately, though unsurprisingly, no medieval moated landscapes survive intact. But there are quite a number of remains, from which some idea can be formed of how a moat worked in gardening terms. Among the most impressive are those at Bodiam Castle in Sussex, Leeds Castle in Kent

CHAPTER FIVE:
WATER

LEFT: *A cascade in the water gardens at Studley Royal, Yorkshire, laid out by the Aislabie family in the 18th century.*

and Windsor Castle in Berkshire. Bodiam, built in 1385 and now owned by the National Trust, is still set within its moat and has a system of pools and dams, the form of which can be traced in the gardens beyond. Leeds Castle is Anglo-Saxon in origin, renewed by Henry VIII as a kind of Tudor hunting lodge: again, of the original gardens only the moat remains. The most famous early moat garden – and one that can still be visited – is at Windsor Castle. This was laid out as a garden from at least the early fifteenth century, when the Scottish Prince James was held prisoner there for a decade. The moat garden lay beneath his quarters, and he described it in his poem 'The King's Quair':

> *Now was there made fast by the tower's wall,*
> *A garden faire, and in the corners set*
> *An arbour green with wandis [slender branches] long and small*
> *Railed about; and so with treis [trees] set*
> *Was all the place, and hawthorn hedges knet,*
> *That life was none, walking there forby,*
> *That might within scarce any wight [person] espy.*

Of the later medieval moats there are interesting examples at Oxburgh and Hunstanton, both in Norfolk, and at Kenilworth in Warwickshire. Oxburgh once lay within marshland, and its moat formed part of an ornamental water garden that survived until the eighteenth century, and that is now being considered for restoration. The moated garden at Hunstanton has been immortalized by P.G. Wodehouse in his story 'Jeeves and the Impending Doom', in which a characteristically irate American millionaire is stranded by Bertie Wooster's young cousin Thomas ('a fiend in human shape'). The laked garden 'stood to the east of the house, beyond the rose garden, and covered several acres. In the middle of it was an island. In the middle of the island was a building known as the Octagon. And in the middle of the Octagon, seated on the roof and spouting water like a public fountain, was the Right Hon A.B. Fillmer.'

Wodehouse stayed more than once at Hunstanton, which dates from 1487; he wrote, precariously, on a typewriter floating on a punt within the moat. Both moat and Octagon survive today. Kenilworth is a great medieval castle, with a pleasance first created by Henry V.

It was given a remarkable makeover in the late sixteenth century by the Earl of Leicester, which included extensive water gardens, one single moat and another double moat.

The ornamental moat fell out of favour with the close of the sixteenth century. A late revival is the medieval moat at Blickling Hall, Norfolk, renewed in 1616. Archive documents show that the Jacobean builders wanted it both for its aesthetic value, and as an outlet for the hall's sewage. Within about fifty years, however, it had been drained and was used as a sheltered garden area for tender plants. It was replanted in the 1930s by the notable garden designer Norah Lindsay.

PONDS

THE SMALL, ORNAMENTAL POND is a creation of the Middle Ages. Usually stocked with fish, the pond's function was both productive and aesthetic: medieval gardens typically have more than one, to separate young fish from adult ones. One of the best recorded is at the royal gardens laid out by Henry III at Woodstock in Oxfordshire. A record from 1250 orders the gardeners 'to make round about the garden of our Queen two walls, good and high, so that no one may be able to enter, with a becoming and honourable herbary near our fish pond, in which the same Queen may be able to amuse herself; – and with a certain gate from the herbary which is next the chapel of Edward our son, into the aforesaid garden'.

Woodstock had a linked series of three ponds, of which the last still survives beside Capability Brown's lake. Fish-ponds are indeed the most common survivals from medieval landscapes – particularly on monastic sites, often otherwise abandoned after the Dissolution (1536–9). The remains of fish-ponds can still be seen at Cirencester Abbey in Gloucestershire, while Newstead Abbey in Nottinghamshire has a well-preserved example. Once called the Mirror Pond, because it was so still and clear, it is more commonly known as the Eagle Pond because the monks at the Dissolution hid beneath its waters a brass eagle lectern containing the monastery's deeds, which was rediscovered in the eighteenth century. After the Dissolution the monastery passed to the Byron family: the poet Lord Byron (1788–1824) buried his favourite dog, Boatswain, beside the Eagle Pond – though given that Boatswain died of rabies, a waterside location was perhaps not the most sensitive choice. Buildwas Abbey in Shropshire had a sequence of four ponds. They were named Purgatory, Hell, the Abbot's

Pond and the Bath Pond. It is not recorded whether the Abbot's Pond and Bath Pond were a step up from Purgatory, or a step down from Hell. They survived into the twentieth century, but have since disappeared, leaving only a rough outline.

James I created fish-ponds in his ornamental vine garden at Westminster, and kept cormorants, ospreys and otters there. By the end of the seventeenth century the word 'pond' usually denoted a fish-pond, as opposed to a purely ornamental feature. As garden layouts grew more architectural, bodies of water tended to be created in geometric forms, such as canals and basins, rather than the humble pond. One notable exception is the Round Pond, a basin created by Charles Bridgeman in Kensington Gardens in 1728. The Round Pond lay at the centre of a formal layout of radiating rides. In the new informal landscape of the eighteenth century, however, there was less call for small areas of water: these had been proportionate to the garden enclosures of earlier centuries, but were less so in wider, more open gardens. A good example of the change can be found at Blickling Hall in Norfolk. The sinuous lake here was excavated in the early eighteenth century on the site of a small square pond that was part of a wilderness garden laid out a century earlier. At first called the New Pond, this much more extensive piece of water was soon renamed the Lake; and ponds no longer formed any part of the ornamental gardens.

Ponds in domestic gardens enjoyed an extraordinary revival in the twentieth century. Stocked with brightly coloured fish and aquatic plants, these really are the modern-day descendants of the medieval pond. Of course, they no longer have a productive function, but they add a great deal to the experience of the garden, without disturbing the physical proportions of a relatively restricted space: In that, they genuinely reanimate the delights of their medieval forebears.

STREAMS & RILLS

THE TERMS 'STREAM' and 'rill' are both applied to small courses of flowing water, so what distinguishes them? Perhaps only the names themselves: 'stream' is an ancient, Anglo-Saxon word, while 'rill' is a sixteenth-century introduction from Dutch. Probably the first time streams were considered seriously as part of the designed landscape was (once again) the early eighteenth century. In an essay in the *Spectator*, Joseph Addison remarked:

...there is a Fountain rising in the upper part of my Garden, which forms a little wandring Rill, and administers to the Pleasure as well as the Plenty of the Place. I have so conducted it, that it visits most of my Plantations; and have taken particular Care to let it run in the same manner as it would do in an open Field, so that it generally passes through Banks of Violets and Primroses, Plats [plots] of Willow, or other Plants, that seem to be of its own producing.

Of course, at the time it was no doubt revolutionary that water might be allowed to follow its own course in the garden (or at least appear to do so) – though as we have already remarked, Addison's own garden was actually rather conventional and formal, so there may be just a little flight of fancy here. Addison seems nevertheless to have started something, and a few years later the most famous rill in English gardens was created. Its creator was William Kent, who was laying out one of his masterpieces at Rousham in Oxfordshire. Rousham makes a wonderfully inventive use of water, and one example of that is the Serpentine Rill that Kent made to wander in curves through woods to arrive at last in the Venus Vale. It can still be seen today, at the heart of an eighteenth-century idyll. Other notable rills, it must be admitted, are few and far between, though there is a good twentieth-century example designed by Edwin Lutyens at Hestercombe in Somerset.

WATERFALLS

WATERFALLS AS GARDEN FEATURES are close in definition to cascades. Indeed, the name 'cascade' is often used for both. Although 'waterfall' might sometimes be thought of as a naturally occurring phenomenon, and 'cascade' as the artificial version, in fact the difference is not so clear-cut. 'Cascade', after all, is derived from the Italian and French words for 'waterfall' – *cascata* and *cascade* – and in English naturally occurring waterfalls are often called 'cascades'. Moreover, the informal, artificial cascades of the eighteenth century and afterwards often look exactly like natural waterfalls. Nonetheless, we keep to an admittedly arbitrary distinction – that waterfalls are indeed the work of nature – with one important exception. The Cup and Saucer waterfall at Erddig in Clwyd is unmistakably artificial and the work of

William Emes, an eighteenth-century landscaper working in the tradition of Capability Brown. The 'cup' is a hole in a large, circular depression – the 'saucer'. The stream flowing into the cup and saucer falls to create a cylindrical waterfall visible through an arch below; it has been restored by the National Trust, who took over the estate in 1973.

Naturally occurring waterfalls form a significant part of the garden layout at Hafod in Wales. It is a fascinating example because it was inherited by Thomas Johnes in 1786, just as the picturesque movement, with its love of rough and rugged landscape, was gathering pace in England. Hafod is perfect material for an admirer of picturesque principles. It is full of deep valleys, waterfalls and cataracts, and Johnes incorporated these into a series of walks around his estate that provided successive 'pictures' to delight the visitor. Johnes's house burnt down in the early nineteenth century, but some of his walks can still be traced and are well worth a visit.

ABOVE: *An early-15th-century woodcut of a Marian garden, complete with guardian angels and central fountain.*

building. And as you punctuate the landscape with the new architecture, it will collectively form an iconography and a kind of architectural narrative. Good examples of this can be seen at Stourhead in Wiltshire and at William Shenstone's The Leasowes in Warwickshire, in which the journeying visitor is led from one architectural metaphor to another, and is successively instructed in just how this landscape is to be read. Garden experience in such cases is much more mobile (even if the spectators themselves were often carried rather than using their own legs), and its architectural structures differ as a result.

These are just two fundamentals to consider when reading garden buildings, but they are among the most important. Space does not permit us to discuss all the other considerations, and neither can we cover every possible variety of garden structure. Of the latter, we've restricted ourselves to around thirty, and these are dealt with in alphabetical order in the following pages.

⊞ BANQUETING HOUSES

A BANQUETING HOUSE is, as its name suggests, a garden building where banquets are held. In this context, however, 'banquet' is used in its older and perhaps original sense, referring not to a great feast, but to a dessert course of sweetmeats, fruit and wine, often served in a different location from the main meal. (In Scotland you might still hear the expression 'a cake and wine banquet'.) As ornamental gardens developed during the sixteenth century, it became fashionable to host dessert courses in them, and larger banqueting houses could provide space for musicians to play for the diners.

The banqueting house is a good example of a garden building designed for socializing, not as a resting place en route to a further destination. It was usually close to the main house – partly so that guests wouldn't have to walk too far, and partly so that food wouldn't have to be carried long distances – and was often in an identical or complementary architectural style to the main house. The size of banqueting houses varied enormously. The one at Blickling in Norfolk, now lost, provided space for a table and a few chairs, while that at Chipping Campden in Gloucestershire, now owned by the Landmark Trust, is a substantial three-storey affair. Banqueting houses of more than one storey typically devote one floor to a kitchen. The surviving examples are usually in brick or stone, but different materials were employed. The royal gardens at Nonsuch in Surrey had a half-timbered example, and for large court entertainments temporary banqueting houses might be erected. The antiquarian John Stowe wrote of a spectacular one made at Whitehall in 1581 'for certaine Ambassadors out of France'. Built near the river, it was round – 332 feet (100 m) in diameter – with a canvas roof painted to resemble clouds. '[T]his house was wrought most cunningly with ivy and holly, with pendants made of wicker rods garnished with bay, rue, and all manner of strange flowers garnished with spangles of gold…' The heyday of banqueting houses was the sixteenth and early seventeenth centuries, but they continued to be built for centuries after: there are eighteenth-century versions at Studley Royal in Yorkshire and at Gibside, near Gateshead, Tyne & Wear.

 ## BRIDGES

WHILE BRIDGES HAVE FORMED ornamental structures within the garden for centuries, the great age of garden bridges in England is the eighteenth century. One of the earliest, and grandest, is the Grand Bridge at Blenheim in Oxfordshire. Built by John Vanbrugh from 1708, and based on designs by Palladio, it is 400 feet (120 m) long, and was originally intended to include arcades and towers rising to 80 feet (25 m). The towers were never completed, but the main body of the bridge contained thirty-three rooms – none of any particular use – and the bridge was so high that it was some years before enough soil could be found to join it to the lower ground each side of the river. Blenheim's Grand Bridge came into its own later in the century when Capability Brown had the ingenious idea of flooding the valley and submerging half of the stonework: suitably reduced in scale, it has provided a dramatic approach to the house ever since. Palladio's designs, however, became the models of choice for bridge builders. There is a gorgeous example at Wilton in Wiltshire, built in 1737 and copying a design by Palladio for the Rialto Bridge in Venice that was never built; the Wilton bridge was itself later copied at Stowe in Buckinghamshire and at Prior Park in Bath. Yet another Palladian bridge was created at Stourhead in 1762 – this one based on the bridge designed by Palladio for Vicenza. Classically inspired bridges were also built by Robert Adam – at Audley End in Essex, for example; whilst chinoiserie pattern books provided inspiration for wooden 'Chinese' bridges, such as those at Painshill in Surrey, Wootton in Oxfordshire, Biddulph in Staffordshire, and over the canal at Godmanchester in Cambridgeshire.

One great attraction of bridges for landscape gardeners is that they can conceal just how far the water extends beyond them: a good example is Walton Bridge at Painshill (1740s), which adeptly conceals the true extent of the lake. The supreme example of this kind of deception is perhaps the late-eighteenth-century bridge at Kenwood House, London, which is not a bridge at all, but a one-sided wooden folly, placed to add interest to the view from the house – a bit like a prop in a theatre, which is precisely what it is.

CAMELLIA HOUSES

CAMELLIAS DO NOT need the protection of camellia houses in order to survive the English climate, but garden owners spent about a hundred years building them under the mistaken impression that they do. It's possible that the first arrivals from China, in the 1730s, were unusually tender, but it's more likely that, coming from exotic climes, camellias were assumed to be averse to the cold. An additional reason for building a camellia house in the eighteenth century was that camellias were not only beautiful but fantastically expensive: if you went to the expense of cultivating them, you would want to show them off in a suitably showy (and secure) building. Among the most important examples are Henry Flitcroft's 1738 camellia house at Wentworth

LEFT: *The camellia was a flower of great prestige – and price – in the 18th century.*

RIGHT: *The screen gates at Hampton Court, London, designed by Jean Tijou in 1698.*

Woodhouse in Yorkshire; Jeffrey Wyatt's creations at Woburn Abbey in Bedfordshire and Bretton Hall in Yorkshire; and Lord Aberconwy's at Bodnant Hall in Conwy.

The death knell for camellia houses was probably rung by the winter of 1838, which was bitingly cold – and which camellias managed to survive. From that time on, camellias – now easier and cheaper to buy – were increasingly grown outdoors.

CLAIRE VOIES

A *CLAIRE VOIE* IS an openwork gate, fence or grille set in a wall at the end of a straight walk or *allée*, which offers a view out of the garden into the wider landscape. It is, as its name suggests, a French invention, and is a consequence of the seventeenth-century French delight in long, straight *allées*. Ending an *allée* with a solid wall or fence spoils the effect entirely, so something that can be seen through has to be placed there instead. In England it was first described in 1712 by John James, who was translating the French gardening writer Dezallier d'Argenville: 'Grills of Iron are very necessary Ornaments in the Lines of Walks, to extend the View, and to shew the Country to Advantage.' They were an important element in the development of the ha-ha (see pages 227–8), when iron bars were thought too emphatic a barrier. Usually they will be found in gardens of the seventeenth century or shortly after, but there are occasional later examples, especially in Arts and Crafts gardens. There are good early examples at Westbury Court in Gloucestershire, and at Castle Howard in Yorkshire, not to mention the extraordinary screen gates at Hampton Court by Jean Tijou (1698), who also designed the screens for St Paul's Cathedral in London.

Cottages Ornées

THE COTTAGE *ORNÉE* is a product of the vagaries of the English class system: partly an attempt by aristocrats at romanticized 'humble' living, partly an attempt by the middle classes to appropriate aristocratic country house comforts. As the *Penny Cyclopaedia* announced in 1845, 'the term cottage has for some time past been in vogue as a particular designation for small country residences and detached suburban houses, adapted to a moderate scale of living, yet with all due attention to comfort and refinement'. In landscape terms this meant small, picturesque houses at which duchesses might not turn up their noses, and the early examples date from the late eighteenth century. Of the surviving examples, the best known are probably Endsleigh in Devon, and the cottages of Blaise Hamlet in Bristol. Endsleigh was

designed by Jeffrey Wyatville in 1811 for the Duke and Duchess of Bedford, with grounds laid out by Humphry Repton. Now a fifteen-room luxury hotel, it is distinctly on the aristocratic end of the scale. Blaise Hamlet, by way of contrast, is a series of nine individually designed cottages around a green, built *c.* 1811 by John Nash for retired employees of John Scandrett Harford, who owned the nearby Blaise Castle; here the emphasis was on providing humble dwellings that would not disgrace a beautiful landscape.

▩ DOVECOTES

SOMETIMES KNOWN AS a 'columbarium' or 'columbary' – from the Latin *columba* (dove) – a dovecote, like a fish-pond, was once a productive requisite in every estate yard or garden. Now there are comparatively few left. Like the vanished fish-ponds, dovecotes are

LEFT: *The Duke of Bedford's Cottage Ornée,*
Endsleigh in Devon: a palatial cottage.
Photograph courtesy of Endsleigh Hotel.

CHAPTER SIX
STICKS AND
STONES
✳

essentially living larders – an excellent source of readily available protein. Prior to the eighteenth century, pigeons were in fact the chief source of winter meat in country houses. One reason for this is the exceptionally short breeding cycle of the bird: an adult pigeon will lay two eggs every six weeks almost throughout the year, and within a month of hatching a young pigeon will be as big as its parent. The birds' droppings were also a valuable fertilizer, and old legal contracts for looking after dovecotes always specify who had rights to the dung. That value was increased still further in the seventeenth century when pigeon droppings became an important source for saltpetre – the essential ingredient in gunpowder manufacture. No surprise, then, that ownership of dovecotes was legally restricted to lords of the manor – nor that, notwithstanding that restriction, over 25,000 were once standing in England, the oldest dating back to Norman days.

Dovecotes come in all shapes and sizes, and it is difficult to generalize about their design, though there is a slight tendency for them to be sited in the lee of the prevailing wind and with a south-facing roof to give the birds a sunny, sheltered resting place. There are noteworthy examples at Rousham in Oxfordshire, standing in a formal garden of clipped box; at Cotehele in Cornwall, dating from the fifteenth century; and at Athelhampton in Dorset, also fifteenth century, which has approximately a thousand nesting holes.

▦ FOLLIES

THE OXFORD ENGLISH DICTIONARY definition of a folly is: 'a popular name for any costly structure considered to have shown folly in the builder'. It's possible, however, that the origin of the name does not lie in stupidity, but derives from the Old French *folie*, which could mean 'delight' – quite a different, but not altogether inappropriate, meaning. Follies are often regarded by definition as conspicuously useless buildings – and that is part of their pleasure – though the reality is a little more complex. Certainly their eccentricity can show a high level of playfulness on the part of their builders, and they often function as elaborate architectural jokes. Within the landscape, however, they also have two distinctive uses. The first is as an eye-catcher or focus for a view – something very common in the eighteenth century. The second is as an advertisement: because the apparent usefulness of the folly is out of proportion to the cost of its construction, follies are a good example of conspicuous

LEFT: *The ruined abbey at Painshill Park, Surrey –*
neither a true ruin nor a true abbey, but a folly built
in the 18th century.

CHAPTER SIX
STICKS AND
STONES
✳

consumption – and an effective means of displaying the wealth and/or architectural knowledge of the owner.

English landscape gardens are full of follies, of an extraordinary variety. Amongst the many possible variants are sham ruins, such as those at Wimpole in Cambridgeshire, Hagley in Worcestershire, and Stowe in Buckinghamshire; towers, such as those at Kew in Surrey and Stourhead in Wiltshire; and arches, such as the appropriately named Eye-catcher designed by William Kent at Rousham in Oxfordshire in the 1730s.

⬚ GARDEN FURNITURE

THE HISTORY OF GARDEN FURNITURE – seats, benches, tables and chairs – could well occupy an entire volume. For the visitor to historic gardens, however, certain points are worth observing. The first is that although garden furniture can be made from a wide range of materials, the most popular material historically has been wood; and wood, as every gardener knows, does not survive indefinitely outdoors. For that reason, the amount of completely

ABOVE: *Garden furniture medieval style: low turfed*
brick seats, in an engraving dating from 1450.

RIGHT: *A simple curving metal seat in the Edwardian garden at Plas Brondanw in Gwynedd, Wales.*

authentic historic furniture in our gardens is comparatively limited. Second, as the introduction to this chapter suggests, the role of garden furniture depends very much on the role played by the garden itself. An Elizabethan or Jacobean garden might have seats on terraces or mounts in order to view the garden; within arbours for meditation and solitude; or within summer-houses or banqueting houses for eating and socializing – and all these indicate a more or less static engagement with the garden. An eighteenth-century landscape garden, by contrast, might have a greater number of seats spread over a greater area. This is because a larger garden that places more emphasis on views makes a visitor's experience of the garden a more mobile one. More seats are required in order to rest during circuits around the garden, and in order to take in the various created views.

Seats in the medieval garden might be wooden, turf or stone. Turf seats (see page 134) fell out of favour in Tudor gardens, but in both periods it was common for seats to be covered, often with some kind of arbour, emphasizing the seat as a place of meditation. The great proliferation of seats during the eighteenth century led John James to write in 1712:

> *…you can scarce ever have too many, there is such a need for them in walking…they look very well also in a garden, when set in certain Places they are destin'd to, as in the Niches or Sinkings that face principal Walks or Vistas, and in the Halls and Galleries of Groves; They are made either of Marble, Free-stone, or Wood, which last are most common; and of these there are two Kinds, the Seats with Backs to them, which are the handsomest, and are usually removed in Winter; and the plain Benches, which are fixed to their Place in the Ground.*

The commonest wooden seat was the Windsor chair, usually painted green (or sometimes white), but as the century progressed, a whole gamut of designs was employed, including Chinese and rustic seats. Native woods, such as beech, lime and oak, were often used, though tropical hardwoods were imported from the mid-eighteenth century. Iron seats were developed towards the end of the eighteenth century, and, being both durable and cheap to produce, remained perennially popular.

 GAZEBOS

A GAZEBO IS A garden building designed to offer views. Although found in seventeenth-century gardens, gazebos were especially popular in that view-loving age, the eighteenth century. Originally the word referred to a turret or lantern offering views from the roof of a house, before being applied to garden buildings. Its etymology is uncertain, but it was coincd by William Halfpenny in *New Designs for Chinese Temples* (1752). Halfpenny (or Michael Hoare, as his real name was) didn't say where he got the word from,

RIGHT: *The extraordinary Vine House at Audley
End, Essex, built in 1802. Note the roots of the vine
extend outside the house, as was normal practice.*

and two suggestions have been made. The first – because Halfpenny was writing about Chinese architecture – was that he must have based it on some unknown oriental term. The second – and more probable – was that he playfully mixed up the Latin *videbo* (I shall see) with the English 'gaze' (a medieval word that has no known etymology). After the eighteenth century the word 'gazebo' spread, first to include any structure that provides views within the garden – from Tudor times to the present day – and then to apply to almost any garden house.

GREENHOUSES, GLASSHOUSES & CONSERVATORIES

'GREENHOUSE' IS A TERM first used in the late seventeenth century. Then, as now, it denoted a building that provided shelter for plants too tender to grow outdoors. It was called 'green' because 'greens' was the name for tender plants. In fact, 'greens' could refer to any plants that kept their foliage all year round; it's possible that the particular association with tenderness arose because quite a number of the popular exotics of the seventeenth century, such as bay and myrtle, would keep their leaves if suitably sheltered. Oxford's Botanic Garden had a house built 'for tender greens' in the late seventeenth century.

The very earliest greenhouses were made from wood, though stone and brick soon became the preferred materials of construction. Unlike today's greenhouses, those of the seventeenth and eighteenth centuries did not employ much glass – partly because glass was expensive, partly because it was taxed, and partly because it was not then available in large sheets. They usually had glass windows on just one, south-facing wall – the classic eighteenth-century orangery is a good example of this.

Greenhouses tended to become larger and to use more glass in the eighteenth century, as the number of exotic imports increased. As these plants were both valuable and fashionable, it was a natural development to locate them near the main house. It is probably this

Who loves a garden, loves a greenhouse too.
WILLIAM COWPER

development that explains the origin of the conservatory. The word 'conservatory' had been used since the early seventeenth century for quite simply anything that needed conserving; this could range from ice, to fish or meat, to water (i.e. a reservoir), to clothes and jewellery, to plants. In the late eighteenth century someone had the bright idea of appending the horticultural version to the house itself. As the *European Magazine* commented in 1782, 'the idea of a Conservatory opening by a folding door into [the] saloon, is too fine to be left unfinished' – and so the modern conservatory was born.

The real breakthrough for greenhouses, however, came in the first half of the nineteenth century, when considerable advances were made in the production of sheet glass, and the tax on windows was lifted. It is from this period that the term 'glasshouse' dates, as the use of glass became more and more widespread. The interior of the greenhouse was also influenced by technological developments. Greenhouses were periodically heated from an early date: Thomas Hanmer in 1659 recommended lighting a fire within on 'violent cold nights', and enquiring seventeenth-century minds were interested in the possibilities of heated plant rooms. Large eighteenth-century greenhouses were heated by fires lit outside the plant room, the heat travelling along flues inside. Others had cast-iron stoves within. But the first piped heating, carrying hot water or hot air, dates from the 1820s.

Developments in plate glass enabled greenhouses to be built on an ever-increasing scale in the nineteenth century: the one at Chatsworth in Derbyshire, for example, had 1 acre (0.4 hectares) of glass, which was heated by Joseph Paxton's Great Stove. Technological advances also explain an explosion in the different types of greenhouse: these included the peach house (or peachery), vine house (or vinery), tomato house, rhododendron house, banana house, camellia house, heath house, geranium house and Australian house. There is a marvellous story associated with banana houses, which doubtless owes its origin to the understandable but sometimes infuriating self-praise exhibited by those who grow their own fruit and vegetables ('Nothing like the shop-bought variety'). At Petworth in Sussex during the nineteenth century Lord Leconfield, having learnt that only home-grown bananas were worth eating, ordered the building of a banana house, and waited impatiently for results. When the first ripe banana was ready, as his grandson later related, it 'was brought in on a lordly dish. My grandfather peeled it with a golden knife. He then cut a sliver off and, with a golden fork, put it in his mouth and carefully tasted it. Whereupon he flung dish, plate, knife, fork and

ABOVE: *The classic use for the garden greenhouse: sheltering tender plants such as these geraniums through the winter months.*

banana to the floor and shouted, "Oh God, it tastes just like any other damn banana!" Banana tree and all were ordered to be destroyed.' The total cost of that banana was estimated at £3000 – roughly £175,000 at today's prices.

Ultimately, the greenhouse is simply an artificial extension of a limited northern hemisphere growing season. The heyday of the domestic greenhouse was the mid- to late twentieth century, when cheap, aluminium-framed houses became widely available. In recent years their popularity has declined as, for example, southern hemisphere bedding plants, such as geraniums, petunias and verbenas, have become mass-produced for garden centres, and as cheap imports of foreign fruit and vegetables fill the supermarkets. But for propagation and shelter of young plants they are still an essential part of the gardener's armoury.

GROTTOES

'GROTTO' COMES FROM *crupta*, the Latin word for 'cave' or 'vault', which in common Roman speech became *grupta*. The modern word owes its existence to the Italian poet Dante Alighieri (1265–1321), who coined the Italian *grotta* in his *Divine Comedy*. Dante's infernal grottoes are often horrific, but sometimes mysteriously inspiring too. This combination of awe and inspiration was irresistible for Italian garden-makers during the Renaissance, who loved to send water dripping through shady caverns containing heroic statues, and encrusted with artificial stalactites, shells, crystals and *tufa* (calcareous formations resembling coral). In a Mediterranean climate these recesses also provided valuable relief from the heat of the sun.

The earliest grottoes in England were, unsurprisingly, created in Italian-influenced gardens, such as those at Nonsuch (*c.* 1580), and the tradition was continued by the Italophile John Evelyn in the seventeenth century. But the grotto in the English garden really belongs to the eighteenth century. The poet Alexander Pope's, created from about 1718, was

LEFT: *The grotto at Painshill Park, Surrey, was*
constructed at great expense by Charles Hamilton in
the 1760s. The stalactites are all man-made.

CHAPTER SIX
STICKS AND
STONES
✸

embellished over the years with gifts – shells, crystals, minerals, marble and stalactites – from a wide circle of friends. Another fine example was constructed by the merchant Thomas Goldney in Bristol, begun in 1737 and filled with shells acquired from West Africa and the West Indies. One of the most spectacular grottoes was built at Painshill Park in the 1760s, where thousands of pieces of spar (a crystalline mineral) were used to create enormous stalactites.

In many ways the grotto represents, quite literally, the dark underbelly of the English landscape garden. Murky, crabbed, intricate, multi-faceted and restless, the grotto is an alter ego for the smooth, light, sinuously Arcadian landscapes of the surface. As the fashion for the rugged, irregular picturesque landscape grew towards the end of the eighteenth century, so the fashion for grottoes below ground diminished. It's worth noting too that if the appearance of grottoes was awe-inspiring, so was their cost. The Earl of Donegall was said in 1788 to have spent £10,000 on shells for his grotto – close to £1 million in today's prices. In addition, grottoes were, and are, notoriously difficult to maintain – as might be expected of any structure designed to permit water to drip through it. A great expense that has to be repeated every few years cannot be indefinitely attractive, especially when fashions change.

Today the grottoes at Goldney and Painshill have been restored, as have others at Goodwood in Sussex and Hampton Court House.

HA-HAS

A HA-HA IS A sunken barrier designed to keep cattle and sheep out of a garden without any visible obstacle. It consists of a ditch, typically perpendicular on the garden side and sloping outwards on the far side, with a wall, fence or hedge placed in the bottom. The first ha-has were French, created in the seventeenth century for a very particular purpose that owes something to the geometric regularity of gardens of the time. When a straight walk or *allée* led to the edge of the formal garden, a wall or fence cutting across formed an unsightly obstacle. To preserve the view outwards, a sunken fence or ha-ha would terminate the walk instead. As for its name: well, as the seventeenth-century gardening writer Dezallier d'Argenville explained, when one reaches the end of such a walk and encounters such a ditch, it 'surprizes…and makes one cry, *Ah! Ah!* from whence it takes its Name'.

The ha-ha revolutionized the English garden. The first example was probably dug at Levens in Cumbria by the French gardener Guillaume de Beaumont in the 1690s, and served the same purpose as the French originals. The simple but significant development was to extend the ha-ha all round the garden so that open views through to parkland could be obtained not just from walks and *allées*, but from any point in the garden. Now ornamental landscape could extend through an entire estate; the ha-ha is a precondition of the English landscape garden. The first large-scale ha-has in England date from the second decade of the eighteenth century: early examples remain at Stowe in Buckinghamshire and at Hackwood in Hampshire. Charles Bridgeman was probably the first landscaper to make widespread use of them.

The ha-ha achieved an extraordinary popularity in the 1730s and 1740s – a period coinciding with the career of William Kent, who, as Horace Walpole said, 'leapt the fence and saw that all was Nature'. Ha-has can be seen in estates all across the country, but the one designed by William Kent at Rousham still stands, and still keeps cattle out of the garden.

⊞ HERMITAGES

THE ORIGIN OF THE garden hermitage is probably the eighteenth century's obsession with all things medieval. That enthusiasm was fanned by the same century's favourite dead poet, John Milton (1608–74), who had spoken approvingly of 'the peaceful hermitage,/ The hairy gown and mossy cell'. As elaborate garden buildings became more popular in the early eighteenth century, it was only a matter of time before mossy hermitages were added to their number – together with, in some cases, suitably hairy occupants. They are typically small, free-standing buildings of rustic construction in rough stone, or timber with a coarse thatched roof. One of the earliest was built around 1731 at Stowe by William Kent, who also built a hermitage for Queen Caroline at Richmond in Surrey. Once royal approval was granted, hermitages began springing up all over the country. A notorious example was the thatched hermitage at Painshill, occupied by a hermit hired by garden owner Charles Hamilton at a fee of 700 guineas for seven years' service. The hermit was expected to wear a camlet robe, never to cut his nails or hair, and never to talk to the servants who brought his food. The successful applicant lasted three weeks, until he was discovered in a local ale-house and dismissed under suspicion of improper relations with a dairy maid. Perhaps mindful of that failure, Sir Rowland Hill of Hawkstone Park in Shropshire populated his hermitage with an automaton called Francis. Henry Hoare, on the other hand, liked to perform the role himself in his hermitage at Stourhead, whilst Gilbert White at Selborne in Hampshire persuaded his brother to take on the job. Unoccupied hermitages have continued to be built in gardens, following the Miltonic idea of secluded study and peace.

HOTHOUSES

THE WORD 'HOTHOUSE' is a generic term for a heated glasshouse, first used in the eighteenth century. In its earlier (sixteenth-century) incarnation it denoted a bath-house, and was also a slang term for a brothel. For more detail on glasshouses, see pages 218–24.

LODGES

WITHIN AN HISTORIC GARDEN or park, lodges come in two basic forms. The first – slightly older – is that of the hunting lodge, which could be a substantial building. The house at Great Fosters in Windsor Forest, Surrey, is a good example of an Elizabethan hunting lodge, whilst New Park Manor in the New Forest, Hampshire, was once Charles II's preferred haunt when out hunting. Both are now hotels, appropriately for buildings that provided accommodation on country trips. Small hunting lodges are also common. Rushden Triangular Lodge in Northamptonshire, is a fascinating variant, built by Sir Thomas Tresham in the late sixteenth century as a warrener's lodge – a warrener being the man who kept and killed rabbits. Tresham's outlawed Catholicism revealed itself in this three-sided building through an astonishingly complex symbolism of the Holy Trinity.

The other form of lodge is that found at the entrance to a park or estate, a term also applied to the entrance of Oxford and Cambridge colleges. In the late eighteenth and early nineteenth centuries, as carriage-borne visitors became more numerous, entrance lodges became more important and elaborate buildings, often setting a keynote for the architectural style of the as yet unseen main house. A good example is the mock-castle lodge at Blaise Castle, Bristol, designed by Humphry Repton.

RIGHT: *The Mount at New College, Oxford, shown in its original stepped pyramidal design in this late seventeenth century engraving. The terraces have since been smoothed over.*

⊞ MOUNTS

MOUNTS ARE ONE of the defining elements of the Tudor and seventeenth-century garden. Outside the garden the word is often used in the period to describe fortifications, and this may in part explain its origins, as a military defence. But the mount is first and foremost a viewing platform. As Francis Bacon explains in his essay 'On Gardens', 'At the End of both the Side Grounds, I would have a Mount of some Pretty Height…to looke abroad into the Fields'. 'Looking abroad' is not the only desideratum: as we have seen, the Tudor garden, with its intricate design, was best viewed from above, and raised ground within the garden was ideal for this. One of the earliest mounts is described by John Leland in his *Itinerary* (1539): a mount 'writen about in degrees like turnings of cokilshells to come to the top without payne'. This spiralling type, for obvious reasons, would come to be known as a 'snail mount', and you can still see two examples dating from the late sixteenth century at Lyveden New Bield in Northamptonshire. Mounts could also be pyramidal, conical, shaped like an inverted bowl, or stepped like an Aztec monument. The mounts illustrated by David Loggan in the late seventeenth century at Wadham College and New College, Oxford, are good examples of these last two. The one at New College was first erected in 1529, and, despite changes over the years, still stands.

Some mounts were of enormous size – Henry VIII's at Hampton Court consumed over a quarter of a million bricks – and many would have buildings erected at their summit. (Henry's had a luxurious three-storey banqueting house.) The use of mounts in humbler gardens is explored by William Lawson, who also gives advice in his 1618 book on their construction: 'set it round with quick [a hawthorn hedge] and lay boughes of trees strangely intermingled, the tops

ABOVE: *The Orangery at Blickling Hall, Norfolk, probably designed in around 1782 by Samuel Wyatt and recently restored complete with orange trees and 18th-century seats.*

inward, with the earth in the middle' – i.e. a skeleton of branches provided the framework for the mount. Lawson also remarked that 'if a river run…under your Mount it will be pleasant… You might sit in your Mount and angle a peckled Trout, sleighty Eel, or some other dainty fish.' With a few notable exceptions – for example, the mount raised in Kensington Gardens in the early eighteenth century – mounts disappeared from our gardens after the seventeenth century.

ORANGERIES

AN ORANGERY IS, of course, a garden building devoted to the cultivation of oranges. The word is French in origin, and the building itself probably a French import. Oranges are not native to Europe, and in France and Italy have for many centuries been sheltered indoors over the winter. The first English gardener successfully to raise oranges was Sir Francis Carew, a courtier of Elizabeth I: he protected his trees in winter with a temporary wooden shelter. It is possible that the first orangery in England was built for Queen Henrietta Maria at Wimbledon in the 1620s. It was called a 'garden house' by Cromwell's men when they assessed the house and garden on taking it over in 1649 (they valued the 42 trees inside at £10 each – about £750 per tree today).

The word 'orangery' was actually quite slow to catch on: John Evelyn (of course) was quick to pick it up, but until the eighteenth century it remained uncommon. Moor Park in Surrey

LEFT: *The Orangery at Belton House, Lincolnshire, designed in typical Regency style around 1820 by the fashionable country house architect James Wyatt.*

BELOW: *Stone flags flanked by perennials in the
garden at Plas Brondanw in Gwynedd, Wales.*
RIGHT: *A flight of stone steps designed by Edwin
Lutyens at Hestercombe, Somerset.*

had an 'orange house', and nearby Woburn Abbey had in 1697 a 'penthouse' – what we would call a 'lean-to' ('pent' coming from the French word for 'slope'). Orangeries, however, became very fashionable in the eighteenth century, and most surviving examples date from that time, including those at Kew in Surrey; Bowood in Wiltshire and Kenwood in London, both designed by Robert Adam; Saltram in Devon; and Mount Edgcumbe in Cornwall. Like other plant houses of the period, orangeries are typically of stone construction (usually with a white finish), and with windows on one, south-facing side.

◈ PATHS & WALKS

GARDEN VISITORS DON'T ALWAYS pay a great deal of attention to where they place their feet, but paths are an important feature of historic gardens. They have to be able to cope with large numbers of visitors – a particular headache for conservationists today, although the problem first arose with the mid-eighteenth century fashion for garden visiting. They also have to be able to cope with the English climate, which is not a new problem either. Roman gardens on the Continent were typically pathed with compacted sand and earth; in Britain gravel was more often used because it drains better and isn't spoilt by our rainfall. The Romans also laid stone slabs on their paths, just as we do. Medieval gardeners laid sand, gravel and stone paths, and sometimes added ornamental tiles. But the great majority of paths in historic gardens that can be visited today were laid with gravel or hoggin (a naturally occurring combination of gravel and clay).

The best type of gravel was hotly debated: John Rea, the seventeenth-century gardening writer, argued in favour of 'catsbrain gravel', which sounds distinctly unappealing, and in fact derives from an orangey-grey clay resembling (apparently) cats' brains. Paths in York stone, an attractive sandstone from Yorkshire quarries, began to be laid from the eighteenth century. Brick and clay pavers became more common in the nineteenth century, and brick-weave paths were particularly popularized by the Arts and Crafts movement.

Retrieving the original look of a garden path is always important for garden restorers. Most gravels, for example, were sourced locally, and with a bit of luck you might find among an estate's archives an old bill recording the name of the person who made the delivery: track down that person's address, and you should be able to trace the source of the original gravel.

PATIOS

THE PATIO IS AN OPEN, inner courtyard to a Spanish or Spanish-American house (*pateo* being the Latin word for 'open'). It is in the historic gardens of such houses that visitors are most likely to encounter a patio – for example, the Patio de los Leones or the Patio de la Acequia in the Generalife at Granada in Spain. Nowadays, many domestic houses in England possess a patio, but the idea took some time to arrive. Until the early twentieth century the word was restricted to Spanish or Spanish-American usage. Then however it began to migrate north through the United States, as Spanish influence increased. From the USA it was an inevitable step eastward across the Atlantic. In 1956 a patio graced the 'House of the Future' at the Ideal Home Exhibition in London; and by the 1970s a patio was an all but essential appendage to new homes – not so much a courtyard now, as a convenient, open-air, paved extension to the house. Associated as it is with the 1970s and with architectural features of that period, such as sliding aluminium doors, the patio in the twenty-first century has begun to fall out of fashion. What it retains of its Spanish heritage is that it remains above all a living space: a patio generally opens out from the living-room, not from the kitchen.

PERGOLAS

A FEATURE TAKEN from Italian gardens – inherited in turn from the gardens of Ancient Rome – the pergola was first defined in English in 1598 by the great Elizabethan translator John Florio as 'an arbour made in gardens, or a bower of vines or other boughs; any kind of close walk covered in leaves or boughs' – a description perfectly comprehensible and appropriate today. In fact, in sixteenth-century English the word could also refer to a balcony or raised seating place that might form part of a hunting lodge or banqueting house. None of

LEFT: *An Elizabethan pergola, built as many are today in order to train vines.*

these survive, however, and for gardeners the first version remains dominant: an open framework of wood covering a walkway or seating area.

Despite this venerable history, pergolas really entered English gardens with the rise of the Anglo-Italian garden at the start of the twentieth century – the age of E.M. Forster's novels, when the English created English homes in Italian palaces, and Italian gardens in England. A good example is Harold Peto's wonderful 90-foot (30-m) pergola at West Dean in Sussex. Today the sixteenth-century Italian style of pergola is a popular accompaniment to areas of decking or, indeed, patios; and with a warming English climate, the growing of vines upon them is as easy as it has ever been.

▨ SHEDS & BOTHIES

'SHED' IS AN OLD ENGLISH WORD of mysterious and ancient ancestry. Appropriately enough, it appears in 1481 in one of the very first books printed in English, by the inventor of printing, William Caxton: 'A yerde…in which was a shadde where in were five grete dogges'. Early garden sheds were indeed usually devoted to livestock: human occupancy came later. The potting-shed, for example, is a Victorian invention.

Sheds are not usually the object of visits to historic houses, although the *Zauberflötenhäuschen*, or Magic Flute House – the shed in which Mozart composed the opera of that name – is a notable

LEFT: *The 70-metre-long
pergola designed by Edwin
Lutyens in 1904 for
Hestercombe, Somerset, and
ornamented with climbing
roses.*

exception. Mozart's example can comfort today's gardeners with the thought that time spent in the shed is rarely time wasted.

The bothy has a more particular historic resonance. Derived from *both*, the Gaelic for 'hut', the bothy 'system' was an unattractive feature of estates in Scotland and the north of England. Unmarried male and female servants were forced to live and sleep in dormitory fashion in separate buildings, with often only rudimentary facilities for cooking, washing and cleaning; in the worst cases up to fifty men would sleep on beds of straw in a single bothy. Despite liberal protests in the mid-nineteenth century, the bothy system persisted into the early years of the twentieth century. It was less common in southern England, though not unknown, and it is still possible to visit bothies in which, for example, young apprentice gardeners would be housed: there is one at Audley End in Essex.

Bothies are often sited against kitchen garden walls to ensure that gardeners are close to their work. Today any small shed where gardeners make their tea (as opposed to storing their tools) will still often be called a bothy.

LEFT: *The kitchen gardens at Audley End, Essex. Young gardeners were housed in a bothy by the garden walls, to keep them close at hand.*
RIGHT: *The 17th century formal garden at Ham House, London, is given a focal point by this marble statue.*

STATUES & HERMS

STATUES ARE A COMMON ORNAMENT of gardens dating from the eighteenth century and after. In Tudor gardens statues were greatly outnumbered by wooden effigies, especially of heraldic beasts. Henry VIII's Hampton Court, for example, possessed an extraordinary range of these: harts, lions, unicorns, greyhounds, hinds, dragons, bulls, antelopes, griffins, leopards, rams, tigers and badgers. These would all have been painted, as indeed was the case for almost all early statuary. The proliferation of stone statues in England was slowed by the lack of proficient sculptors. Nicholas Stone (1586–1647), who was master mason to James I and Charles I in turn, was a rare exception: most sculptors at the start of the seventeenth century were immigrants, often Flemish. By around 1680 statues were coming to be seen as appropriate centrepieces for formal gardens, but their popularity reached its zenith in the following century. A comment by the landscape gardener Stephen Switzer is typical: 'That noble Grace that abundance of these Figures, placed all over our Rural Gardens and Plantations, will afford, is charming to consider'.

Statues gave more depth to the experience of the garden, adding a layer of classical iconography. Batty Langley devoted pages of his *New Principles of Gardening* (1728) – a handbook for the new landscape gardens taking shape – to the different statues suitable for

CHAPTER SIX
STICKS AND
STONES

LEFT: *A statue of Hermes provides an eyecatcher at the end of a tree-lined walk at Groombridge Place, Kent.*

BELOW: *This statue is partly concealed in the shade
of the garden at Crook Hall, Durham, imparting an
air of mystery.*

different situations: '*For Fruit-Gardens and Orchards: Pomona* Goddess of Fruit… *For Flower-Gardens: Flora* and *Chloris*, Goddesses of Flowers… *For Mounts, high Terrace-Walks, &c. Aeolus*, God of the Winds and *Orcedes* Fairies of the Mountains…' Good examples of the eighteenth-century enthusiasm for statuary can still be seen in many places, including Chatsworth in Derbyshire and Chiswick in London. William Mason's comment quoted above dates from the 1770s, and illustrates the limits of that enthusiasm: with the ascendancy of the pastoral smoothness of Capability Brown's landscapes, statues ironically began to seem artificial. Their decline is encapsulated by the musings of Squire Headlong in Thomas Love Peacock's *Headlong Hall* (1816):

> *Neptune has been lying these three years in the dust-hole; Atlas had his head
> knocked off to make him prop up a shed; and only the day before yesterday
> we fished Bacchus out of the horse-pond.*

The use of statues is a dangerous attempt in gardening

WILLIAM MASON

Although statues continued to play a part in Victorian gardens, their return to popularity only really began in the twentieth century with the creation of dedicated sculpture gardens, such as the Yorkshire Sculpture Park, and with contemporary versions of eighteenth-century iconographic landscapes, as in Ian Hamilton Finlay's Little Sparta in Lanarkshire.

'Herm' is a Latinized form of Hermes, the messenger of the gods. A herm takes the form of a pillar the height of a man, topped with a bust. These busts on pillars were originally images of Hermes, and were common in ancient Greece as boundary marks, milestones and signposts. They were erected in English gardens of the seventeenth and eighteenth centuries, and can still be seen in many, such as those at Chiswick House.

STONE CIRCLES

STONE CIRCLES ARE an intriguing part of England's ancient landscape. Within our gardens, however, they have a more recent history. The eighteenth century was fascinated by the past: at first this meant primarily Ancient Rome, but as a sense of national identity developed, Britain's own history became a fashionable subject of inquiry. After scholars had investigated the stone circles at Stonehenge and Avebury in Wiltshire for the first time in the early eighteenth century, it was not long before garden owners had the idea of incorporating stone circles and other ancient monuments into the ornamental landscape – or, indeed, of creating their own. One of the most interesting is the Druid's Temple at Park Place in Oxfordshire. This is an authentic ancient circle that originally stood on a hillside above St Helier, Jersey. After the island's governor, General Conway (a keen antiquarian), successfully defended Jersey against the French in 1781, the island's assembly voted to give him the stone circle – whereupon he had it transported across the Channel to England, and erected in his own garden.

Other examples include the Druid's Temple at Piercefield in Gwent, which may be an authentic ancient monument incorporated into the picturesque landscape laid out by Valentine Morris from 1753 (now in a state of near-complete neglect), and the burial chamber at Plas Newydd in Anglesey, another ancient monument, this time landscaped by Humphry Repton. New Swinton Hall, near Ilton in Yorkshire, has a stone circle created by the garden's owner William Danby around 1820. Despite the circle's youth and inauthenticity, visitors at night still report spooky goings-on – which probably says more about the visitors than it does about the stones.

SUMMER-HOUSES

A SUMMER-HOUSE can be defined simply as a garden building that provides shade and relief from hot weather. Often it will be of simple or even rustic construction. Grander versions are usually given grander names – temples, pavilions, gazebos and suchlike – so the summer-house has generally remained the preserve of humbler, domestic gardens. It is distinctly an English invention: only in our climate would summer be singled out as the one time when shade and shelter would be desirable, and there is no comparable, seasonal word in French, Italian or Spanish. In Tudor times and later, the term 'summer-house' could also refer to the countryside home used by aristocratic families when they left London and the Court during the hot months of summer.

SUNDIALS

SUNDIALS HAVE BEEN part of the English designed landscape for a surprisingly long time. One of the oldest in the country is also among the most beautiful: the Bewcastle Cross in Cumbria incorporates a vertical dial and is an extraordinary piece of Anglo-Saxon craftsmanship dating from the late seventh century. Although we typically think of garden sundials as horizontal circles, there are as many designs of dial as there are ways of casting a shadow. Most, however, use a gnomen or stylus to cast a shadow on a surface marked with the hours. The time shown by the dial is called apparent solar time, which – because of the tilt of the Earth's axis and the variations in speed with which the Earth travels round the sun – has to be corrected to obtain the local clock time. If you live in Greenwich (or on the 0° line of longitude), this local time will be the same as Greenwich Mean Time; if not, you will have to add four minutes for every degree west of Greenwich, or subtract four minutes for every degree east. Ipswich, for example, is four minutes behind Greenwich, while Bristol is ten minutes ahead. Historically, sundials were incredibly useful because until the advent of the railways and the corresponding need to standardize times and timetables across the country, local clock time was all that mattered.

Henry VIII had seven sundials in his Privy Gardens at Hampton Court (*c.* 1530). These have since disappeared, but Corpus Christi College, Oxford, still possesses an elaborate pillar sundial in the place of one originally erected in 1579. One of the earliest original dials still standing is the obelisk dial in Drummond Castle, Perthshire, which dates from 1630. Sundials

BELOW: *An armillary sundial in the garden at The Laskett, Herefordshire. The metal rings represent the circles of the celestial sphere.*

CHAPTER SIX
STICKS AND
STONES
❀

were a popular feature of the iconographically minded sixteenth and seventeenth centuries: the one at Llanerch in Denbighshire (*c.* 1660) was inscribed thus:

> *Alas! My friend, time will soon overtake you;*
> *And if you do not cry, by G–d I'll make you.*

It squirted water in the face of the onlooker, just to make sure. Although Henry VIII's dials have vanished, there is still a marvellous example from 1700 at Hampton Court. Other notable

LEFT: *The Temple of Ancient Virtue at Stowe, Buckinghamshire: part of the templescape laid out, aptly enough, by Earl Temple.*

CHAPTER SIX
STICKS AND
STONES
❁

eighteenth-century dials include the one at Squerryes Court in Kent, the pillar dial at Houghton Hall in Norfolk, and the extraordinary polyhedral (multi-faced) dial at Penshurst Place in Kent.

The nature of the dial is limited only by the ingenuity of its designer. More than one Oxbridge college had a garden sundial formed from topiary; Ascott House in Buckinghamshire still possesses its topiary dial with a yew stylus, created in 1902 after the marriage of the gardens' owners and bearing the motto 'Light and shade in turn, but love always'. Sundials are still being created for contemporary gardens: a popular version is the 'human stylus,' in which the spectator tells the time by casting his or her own shadow from a marked spot.

▨ TEMPLES

TEMPLES ARE ONE of the defining buildings of the English landscape garden. There is much debate over which was the first to be created, but the men responsible were probably Charles Bridgeman and John Vanbrugh, who collaborated on gardens at Eastbury in Dorset and Stowe in Buckinghamshire in the early 1720s. Vanbrugh also designed the Temple of the Four Winds at Castle Howard and the Ionic Temple at Duncombe Park (both in Yorkshire) at about the same time. Once the templescape at Stowe, in particular, began to take shape, temple-building became a nationwide craze. Why temples began to be built in gardens is difficult to say. One general influence was the fashion for paintings by the seventeenth-century French artist Claude, who painted idealized landscapes in which temples and ruins featured strongly. Another was the fashion for the civilization and architecture of classical Rome; another, the fashion for the designs of the sixteenth-century Italian architect Andrea Palladio, himself inspired by classical Roman models. (When Vanbrugh worked at Castle Howard, he argued specifically in favour of 'an Italian building', rather than a Roman one.)

Particular credit, however, ought to be given to the owner of Stowe – Viscount Cobham. His family name was Temple, and the family motto was *Templa quam dilecta* (How lovely are your temples). For a garden-lover and architectural connoisseur, as Cobham was, the building of temples probably came naturally; by the time he died in 1749 he had built nearly forty of them. Stowe was widely visited and admired by Cobham's contemporaries: it may be that, having seen just how successful he had been in realizing on the ground the kind of Arcadian landscapes painted by artists such as Claude, they simply wanted to follow suit. With Stowe, a temple became an essential part of the new landscape garden, and in the mid-eighteenth century there were few redeveloped gardens that did not include one. One irony sometimes overlooked is that temples are of course in origin religious buildings: the thousands built in the eighteenth century are almost uniquely architectural and aesthetic delights – a secular indulgence that reflects the economic and military confidence of a period glad to leave behind the religious divisions of the previous century.

Throughout the eighteenth and nineteenth centuries temple design diversified. James Stuart's Temple of Theseus at Hagley (1758), for example, with its baseless Doric columns and other details copied from ancient Greek temples, marks the beginning of the 'Greek revival' in England. Rustic temples were also popular: in the 1780s, Dr Edward Jenner, of smallpox vaccination fame, built a thatched Temple of Vaccinia in his Gloucestershire garden, with a doorway and arch made from two pollarded tree trunks. Others varieties include Chinese temples, of which there is a spectacular example at Biddulph in Staffordshire (1842–56), and Japanese temples, such as the Shinto-inspired example at Tatton Park in Cheshire, built by Japanese workers on a small island in 1910.

▨ TERRACES

AS ARCHITECTURAL STRUCTURES within the garden, terraces probably owe their creation to the Elizabethans. In the late sixteenth century, Italian gardens exercised a small but significant influence in England, and it is quite possible that the terracing of gardens such as the Villa d'Este at Tivoli (itself based on Roman originals) prompted English imitations. The first notable example in England is in the gardens at Kenilworth Castle in Warwickshire, which were given a spectacular makeover in time for Queen Elizabeth's visit in 1575. The gardens were viewed from a great terrace later described by Robert Laneham, a courtier present at the party: '...hard all along the Castl wall iz reared a pleazaunt Terres of a ten foot hy and a twelve brode: even under foot and fresh of fyne grass'. Kenilworth's terrace performed three important functions: it helped people to see the views; it added structure to the garden; and it was pleasant to walk on. This last point was picked up by Francis Bacon, who advised gardeners to build 'A tarrasse for a wandring and variable minde, to walke up and downe'.

A good example of the early terrace as a viewing platform was created at Wilton in Wiltshire 'for the more advantage of beholding these platts' – in other words, for looking down on the knots below. Queen Henrietta Maria's garden at Wimbledon in the early seventeenth century had a fine turfed terrace planted with lime trees, a feature later copied at other gardens around the country. An example of the more spectacular, Italianate terrace was created by John Evelyn for the Earl of Arundel at Albury in Surrey, still intact today, and occasionally open to visitors. William Cobbett visited in 1822 and described the terrace as 'the most beautiful thing that I ever saw in the gardening way'.

ABOVE: *High walls surrounding the gardens at
Haddon Hall, Derbyshire, with massive buttresses
built to cope with the steeply sloping site.*

In the eighteenth century the viewing possibilities of the terrace predominated. Those at
Duncombe and Rievaulx (both in Yorkshire) are good examples. Alexander Pope enormously
admired the terraces at Sherborne in Dorset, whilst Stephen Switzer filled his ideal garden
designs with 'Terras-walks'. There was still place, however, for Bacon's pacing: as Pope's
friend Lady Mary Wortley Montagu wrote, 'The terrace is my place consecrated to
meditation.' Towards the end of the century the geometry of the terrace fell out of favour, but
terraces returned in the mid-nineteenth century with the development of 'historical'
gardening. They could (and can) be seen in restorations at Hatfield in Hertfordshire and
Montacute in Somerset, and in new gardens influenced by Renaissance Italy at Trentham in
Staffordshire and Shrublands in Suffolk, both designed by Charles Barry (1795–1860). As his
contemporary Thomas Dick Lauder observed, 'the old system of having nothing but shaven
grass, and bare gravel around the house [is] fast giving way to the introduction of walled or
balustraded terraces, and all the rich decorations of the old gardens' – so fashion turns about.
Today there are proposals to restore the gardens at Kenilworth, and visitors may yet be able
to walk in Robert Laneham's steps down the great Elizabethan terrace there.

▣ TRELLIS

THE WORD 'TRELLIS' comes from the Latin *trilicius*, which means 'three-threaded'.
Originally used of cloth, it came to apply to things woven of iron or gold wire, and eventually
to anything woven in a lattice-like arrangement. 'Trelys' in the fifteenth century meant a
lattice placed in front of a window. Although a kind of trellis for training plants might be
used in medieval gardens, the life of the trellis we recognize today actually started in the early
eighteenth century, when it would also be known as 'treillage' (from the French version), or
simply as 'trellis-work'. Since medieval times, however, trellis has been employed to support
climbers, usually vines. In the eighteenth century it was in particular demand as a means of
training fruit trees.

Not merely a support, trellis has always had an ornamental function, and was used from
early times to provide screens around seats, just as it is today. In fact, trellis is one of the great
continuums of English gardening: a trellis supporting a climbing plant around a seat in a
suburban back garden has an ancestry stretching back centuries.

WALLS & FENCES

ALTHOUGH BRICKS WERE MADE and used by the Romans, the use of brick in Britain seems to have died out after the Roman occupation. It gradually returned in the late Middle Ages, but was expensive at first and used only for buildings of high status. Brick walls began to be much more common in the seventeenth century, and can be dated by their size and by the pattern in which they are laid. Early brickwork tends to use 'English bond', in which one course (line) of bricks is laid as stretchers (lengthways), and the next laid as headers (widthways). In 1623 'Flemish

LEFT: *An example of Flemish bond brickwork, probably the earliest in England, dating from 1623 at Blickling Hall, Norfolk.*

bond' was introduced, in which headers and stretchers alternate in the same course: if you see a wall using this bond, it cannot be older than 1623. You may also find several other types of bond used in garden walls: 'English garden wall bond' has courses of headers with three courses of half-lapped stretchers between them; 'Flemish garden wall bond' (also known as 'Sussex bond') has three stretchers between single headers in each course; and 'Rat trap bond' (also known as 'Chinese bond') has the bricks laid on their edge, leaving a cavity (or 'rat trap') between them.

Bricks from the seventeenth century and before are thinner than their modern counterparts – usually about 50 mm (2 inches) across. Although there were attempts to standardize brick size in the seventeenth century, this only really took effect with the mass-production techniques of the nineteenth century: in 1840 the 'Imperial' brick of 9 x 4½ x 3 inches (23 x 11.5 x 7.5 cm) became the standard. Other nineteenth-century innovations include yellow 'London Stock' bricks, and yellowish or grey gault (clay-based) bricks, though red brick was the brick of choice in many Arts and Crafts buildings.

Drystone walls are traditionally used on parkland and agricultural land. Because they have no mortar, they are actually more resistant to decay than bonded walls. The material used for them is whatever is available locally: in the Cotswolds, for example, this will be a golden Jurassic limestone. In Wales, where slate predominates, a typical alternative to the drystone wall is the slate hedge. This is built in a herringbone fashion, with each layer sloping in the opposite direction to its neighbours above and below. In areas where there is little surface stone available, earth banks may be more common than walls, and these may additionally be stone-faced, or have a hedge planted along the top.

In Elizabethan gardens and parks the chief boundary division was the quickset (hawthorn) hedge (see page 81). But parkland was often surrounded by a park pale, which typically took

LEFT: *Wattle fences surround a medieval homestead pictured in a book of 1495.*

the form of a bank and ditch topped by a wooden stake or pale fence high enough to keep deer inside. The pales were made of oak or chestnut poles around 6 inches (15 cm) in diameter. Few of these pales remain, although that around the deer park at Charlecote Park in Warwickshire is estimated to be over 400 years old. Legend has it that Shakespeare went poaching at Charlecote as a youth, so it may have been this very fence that he climbed over.

Of the historic fencing still in common use today, the most familiar form is the post and rail, in which posts are joined by (usually) three wooden rails, to a height of around 3 feet (1 m). The traditional woods used are oak and chestnut, though modern variants use treated softwoods.

Temporary fences, for penning sheep for example, are formed from hurdles. There are two types of these. Wattle hurdles are woven, in a technique similar to that used in basket-making, from coppice rods of hazel. They are one of the oldest forms of fence, and were also used in the construction of huts and houses. (Wattles were fixed to timber frames and the gaps were filled with a mixture of clay and straw – the origin of the term 'wattle and daub'.) Gate hurdles are made from sweet chestnut, ash, oak, elm, hazel or willow. They look like traditional gates, with five or six horizontal rails fixed to an upright at each end, and a couple of diagonals braced across the middle.

Iron fencing became popular in the nineteenth century, and typically imitated the traditional post and rail design, replacing the wide rails with narrow iron struts. In the mid-twentieth century a great deal of parkland fencing and hedging was replaced with post and wire fences, wire netting fences and electric fences. Today, however, farmers are encouraged to restore traditional boundary forms.

CHAPTER SEVEN

DEPARTING

WHEN WE LEAVE A GARDEN, of whatever period and history, a variety of questions presents itself to us. Some are human and practical: *How long will it take to get home? What are we going to have for supper?* Some, though, are more garden-specific, and it is with these that we take our own leave of you.

DID THE GARDEN WORK AS A WHOLE?

When the National Trust approaches the conservation of a garden, one of the first questions it asks is how the 'spirit of place' can be defined. Does the garden possess a distinctive and overriding character into which the many individual elements are subsumed? To take one example: Chatsworth in Derbyshire is a garden that has been subject to developments of a radically different nature through the centuries. The end result is impressive, refreshing, always diverting – but to our minds the garden in its modern incarnation doesn't really hang together as a whole: the constituent parts are just too different. Of course, that may not be a problem in Chatsworth's case, or, indeed, in any

LEFT: *The geometrically cut yew hedges at Great Dixter, Sussex, echo the rooflines of the house in a classic example of Arts & Crafts design.*

other – but the great gardens do tend to possess an almost tangible character that presses itself upon the visitor. How did it work for you?

WHAT DIFFERENCES HAVE THE CHANGES OF HISTORY MADE?

Most historic gardens, as we have seen, are a patchwork of different periods, incorporating changes and developments made by gardeners of different centuries. It's always worth asking how those developments have affected the garden as a whole. Had your visit taken place at another point in history – say, fifty or a hundred years ago – would the garden's effect have been the same? Would it have looked any better, or worked more effectively? Would you have liked it more?

DID I VISIT IN THE RIGHT SEASON?

A key question, this: would we learn more by returning in three months' or six months' time? The idea of a winter garden is a comparatively modern one, but Victorian gardeners, for instance, were adept at extending the seasonal interest of their gardens, and the crisp sculptural lines of a seventeenth-century formal garden may look best of all in the low light of a winter frost.

HOW DOES IT COMPARE TO OTHER GARDENS?

Our old university tutor used to quote to us T.S. Eliot's dictum: 'Comparison and analysis are the chief tools of the critic'. We don't suggest that you need to become a garden critic – nor would we claim to be critics ourselves – but a critical eye, in the best and positive sense of an informed and discerning appreciation, can only be of benefit to the garden experience. Comparing one parterre, terrace or wilderness with another helps us understand not only how they look and function, but why the original gardener created them in the first place.

WHAT CAN I BRING BACK TO MY OWN GARDEN?

In the first instance this may be simply a plant. Many historic gardens open to the public have plant sales of some kind, even if it is just a few pots on a trestle table by the entrance. The great advantage of this is that if a plant catches your eye when walking around the garden, you can buy a cutting before you forget. And, of course, you will have seen how it looks and grows on the ground: a visit to the garden centre is always enjoyable, but there is nothing like seeing a plant *in situ* to help us realize what additions we might make to our own gardens.

❋

Beyond the plants you can carry away, there are the less tangible but potentially just as fertile ideas. Perhaps you can adapt or replicate a specific layout, or a particular arrangement of plants and colours. No one is going to re-create an English landscape garden with eye-catchers and open views in a suburban backyard. But one of the great benefits of the growth in garden history scholarship over the past few decades has been the rediscovery of those earlier ages of gardening. For 600 years, from the twelfth to the seventeenth century, garden masters were working ingeniously with plants in small, geometric, walled and fenced gardens. All the inspiration is there if only we look for it. And if those earlier gardeners can show us how to use an essentially restricted space, we have an immeasurable advantage in the range and palette of plants available to us.

WHERE CAN I LEARN MORE?

First and foremost, ask the gardeners. Those who work in historic gardens have a wonderfully intimate knowledge of the plants and spaces entrusted to them, and our experience is that they are only too willing to share that knowledge.

Then there are the various societies devoted to historic gardens – chief amongst them, the Garden History Society – and the various garden trusts that are now established in most, if not all, English counties. A visit to the Museum of Garden History in London is also instructive.

Finally, there is a wide and growing range of literature devoted to historic gardens, of which we list just a few examples in the section titled Further Reading, overleaf.

WHERE CAN I GO NEXT?

This is the most important question of all. Garden historians used to do their work in libraries and archives, or in their own studies. Nowadays we recognize that the best source for learning about gardens is the gardens themselves. The philosophy of *How to Read an English Garden* is that we discover most from gardens by experiencing and enjoying more of them. In our closing pages we add a brief gazetteer of some of the gardens mentioned. Put the book down, and go out and read the gardens!

APPENDICES

FURTHER READING

Brent Elliott, *Victorian Gardens* (Batsford, London, 1986)
Jane Fearnley-Whittingstall, *The Garden: An English Love Affair* (Weidenfeld & Nicolson, London, 2002)
Miles Hadfield, *A History of British Gardening* (Hamlyn, London, 1969)
John Harvey, *Medieval Gardens* (Batsford, London, 1981)
David Jacques, *Georgian Gardens* (Batsford, London, 1983)
Sylvia Landsberg, *The Medieval Garden* (British Museum, London, 1995)
Timothy Mowl, *Gentlemen and Players: Gardeners of the English Landscape* (Sutton Publishing, Stroud, 2000)
Jenny Uglow, *A Little History of British Gardening* (Chatto & Windus, London, 2004)

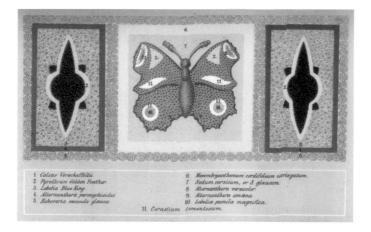

LEFT: *A mighty Wellingtonia, planted in 1861 at Blickling Hall, Norfolk.*

GAZETTEER

KEY: EH = English Heritage; NT = National Trust

ATHELHAMPTON HOUSE
Athelhampton, Dorchester, Dorset DT2 7LG
Tel: 01305 848363
One of the best examples of an Arts and Crafts garden, laid out to accompany a fifteenth-century house. Open March to October.

AUDLEY END HOUSE (EH)
Saffron Walden, Essex CB11 4JG
Tel: 01799 522842/522399
Jacobean house with gardens developed by Capability Brown, Humphry Repton and W.S. Gilpin. Open April to October.

BADMINTON HOUSE
Badminton, Tetbury, Gloucestershire GL9 1DD
Tel: 01454 218346
Vast, formal parkland first laid out in seventeenth century. Park open all year round.

BIDDULPH GRANGE (NT)
Biddulph, Stoke-on-Trent, Staffordshire ST8 7SD
Tel: 01782 517999
Exuberant high Victorian garden of varying styles. Open March to December.

BLAISE CASTLE
Henbury Road, Henbury, Bristol BS10 7QS
Tel: 0117 903 9818
Humphry Repton's most rugged and dramatic landscape. Open all year round.

BLENHEIM PALACE
Woodstock, Oxfordshire OX20 1PX
Tel: 08700 602080
Vanbrugh's palace felicitously surrounded by Capability Brown's parkland. Open February to December.

BLICKLING HALL (NT)
Blickling, Norwich, Norfolk NR11 6NF
Tel: 01263 738030
Jacobean 'prodigy' house with outstanding gardens redesigned by Norah Lindsay in the 1930s. Open all year round.

BOUGHTON HOUSE
Boughton, Kettering, Northamptonshire NN16 9UP
Tel: 01536 515731
Late seventeenth-century Dutch-influenced house and gardens. Open August.

BUSCOT PARK (NT)
Faringdon, Oxfordshire SN7 8BU
Tel: 0845 345 3387
Early twentieth-century Anglo-Italian garden by Harold Peto. Open April to September.

CANONS ASHBY HOUSE (NT)
Canons Ashby, Daventry, Northamptonshire N11 3SD
Tel: 01327 861900
Beautifully preserved early eighteenth-century garden. Open March to December.

CASTLE HOWARD
York, North Yorkshire YO60 7DA
Tel: 01653 648444
Dramatic eighteenth-century landscape garden inspired by ancient Rome. Open March to October.

CHATSWORTH
Bakewell, Derbyshire DE45 1PP
Tel: 01246 565300
Seventeenth-century gardens overlaid with eighteenth- and nineteenth-century developments by Capability Brown and Joseph Paxton. Open March to October.

CHELSEA PHYSIC GARDEN
66 Royal Hospital Road, London SW3 4HS
Tel: 020 7352 5646
Late seventeenth-century formal garden. Open
April to October.

CHENIES MANOR
Chenies, Buckinghamshire WD3 6ER
Tel: 01494 762888
Wonderful Arts and Crafts garden accompanying a
Tudor House. Open April to October.

CHISWICK HOUSE
Burlington Lane, London W4 2RP
Tel: 020 8995 0508
Very influential early eighteenth-century garden.
Open all year round.

CLAREMONT LANDSCAPE GARDEN (NT)
Portsmouth Road, Esher, Surrey KT10 9JG
Tel: 01372 467806
Important and very beautiful early landscape
garden. Open all year round.

CLIVEDEN (NT)
Taplow, Maidenhead, Buckinghamshire SL6 0JA
Tel: 01628 605069
Good example of Sir Charles Barry's mid-Victorian
Italianate style. Open March to December.

CRANBORNE MANOR
Cranborne, Dorset BH21 5PS
Tel: 01725 517289
Tradescant garden replanted in Arts and Crafts style
in the twentieth century. Open Wednesdays, March
to September.

DUNHAM MASSEY (NT)
Altrincham, Cheshire WA14 4SJ
Tel: 0161 941 1025
Eighteenth-century garden with Edwardian
additions. Open March to October.

DYRHAM PARK (NT)
Dyrham, nr Chippenham, Gloucestershire SN14 8ER
Tel: 0117 9372501
Late seventeenth-century house, garden and deer
park. Open March to October.

EDZELL CASTLE
Edzell, Brechin, Angus DD9 7UE
Tel: 01356 648631
Formal gardens of the early twentieth century, laid
out to complement an ancient Scottish castle. Open
all year round.

ELVASTON CASTLE
Elvaston, Derby, DE72 3EP
Tel: 01332 571342
Remains of one of the most prodigious Victorian
gardens. Open all year round.

ERDDIG HALL (NT)
Wrexham, Clwyd, North Wales LL13 0YT
Tel: 01978 355314
Eighteenth-century house with parkland by William
Emes. Open March to December.

FISHBOURNE ROMAN PALACE
Salthill Road, Fishbourne, Chichester, West Sussex
PO19 3QS
Tel: 01243 785859
Roman villa with reconstructed garden. Open
February to December.

GREAT DIXTER
Northiam, Rye, East Sussex TN31 6PH
Tel: 01797 252878
Renowned Arts and Crafts-based gardens by
Christopher Lloyd. Open April to October.

HAM HOUSE (NT)
Ham Street, Ham, Richmond, Surrey TW10 7RS
Tel: 020 8940 1950
Formal seventeenth-century gardens by the banks of
the Thames. Open all year round.

HAMPTON COURT PALACE
East Molesey, Surrey KT8 9AU
Tel: 08707 527777
The greatest royal gardens, redeveloped by successive
monarchs since Henry VIII. Open all year round.

HARDWICK HALL (NT)
Doe Lea, Chesterfield, Derbyshire S44 5QJ
Tel: 01246 850430
Bess of Hardwick's Elizabethan house with formal
gardens. Open March to October.

HATFIELD HOUSE
Hatfield, Hertfordshire AL9 5NQ
Tel: 01707 287010
Jacobean prodigy house with gardens lovingly restored in the late twentieth century. Open March to September.

HESTERCOMBE
Cheddon Fitzpaine, Taunton, Somerset TA2 8LG
Tel: 01823 413923
Edwin Lutyens' and Gertrude Jekyll's masterpiece, recently restored. Open all year round.

HEVER CASTLE
Hever, Edenbridge, Kent TN8 7NG
Tel: 01732 865224
Moated Tudor castle, with Italianate early twentieth-century gardens. Open March to November.

HIDCOTE MANOR (NT)
Hidcote Bartrim, nr Chipping Campden, Gloucestershire GL55 6LR
Tel: 01386 438333
Magical, ground-breaking early twentieth-century gardens. Open March to October.

HOUGHTON HALL
Houghton, King's Lynn, Norfolk PE31 6UE
Tel: 01485 528569
Robert Walpole's monstrous Palladian house, with recently restored kitchen gardens. Open March to September.

IFORD MANOR
Bradford on Avon, Wiltshire BA15 2BA
Tel: 01225 863146
Masterful early twentieth-century Anglo-Italian garden by Harold Peto. Open May to September.

KENILWORTH CASTLE
Kenilworth, Warwickshire CV8 1NE
Tel: 01926 852078
One of the great Elizabethan palaces and gardens, now planned for restoration. Open all year round.

KINGSTON LACY (NT)
Wimborne Minster, Dorset BH21 4EA
Tel: 01202 883402
Seventeenth-century house with formal Victorian gardens. Open all year round.

THE LEASOWES
Leasowes Lane, off Mucklow Hill, Halesowen B62 8DH
Tel: 01384 814642
Shenstone's *ferme ornée*, now undergoing restoration. Open all year round.

LEVENS HALL
Kendal, Cumbria LA8 0PD
Tel: 01539 560321
Late seventeenth-century formal gardens with topiary, faithfully restored in the early nineteenth century. Open April to October.

LITTLE SPARTA
Dunsyre, Lanarkshire, ML11 8NG
Tel: 01556 640244
Iconographic twentieth-century garden by poet Ian Hamilton Finlay. Open June to September.

LONGLEAT
Warminster, Wiltshire BA12 7NW
Tel: 01985 844400
Elizabethan house with gardens reworked by Russell Page in the twentieth century. Open all year round.

LYVEDEN NEW BIELD (NT)
nr Oundle, Peterborough, Northamptonshire PE8 5AT
Tel: 01832 205358
Fascinating remnants of an abandoned Elizabethan garden. Open all year round.

MELBOURNE HALL
Melbourne, Derbyshire DE73 1EN
Tel: 01332 862502
The best surviving example of a London and Wise layout. Open April to September.

MONTACUTE HOUSE (NT)
Montacute, nr Yeovil, Somerset TA15 6XP
Tel: 01935 823289
Beautiful late sixteenth-century house surrounded by formal gardens. Open all year round.

MUNSTEAD WOOD
Heath Lane, Busbridge, Godalming, Surrey
Tel: 01483 417867
Gertrude Jekyll's home and garden. Open for
charity three days a year.

NYMANS (NT)
Handcross, nr Haywards Heath, West Sussex
RH17 6EB
Tel: 01444 400321
Early twentieth-century plantsman's garden. Open
all year round.

OXBURGH HALL (NT)
Oxborough, King's Lynn, Norfolk PE33 9PS
Tel: 01366 328258
Formal gardens and woodland surrounding a late
medieval moated manor house. Open March to
October.

UNIVERSITY OF OXFORD BOTANIC GARDEN
Rose Lane, Oxford, Oxfordshire OX1 4AZ
Tel: 01865 286690
Early seventeenth-century walled gardens by the
banks of the Thames in Oxford. Open all year
round.

PACKWOOD HOUSE (NT)
Lapworth, Solihull, Warwickshire B94 6AT
Tel: 01564 783294
Sixteenth-century house and gardens restored in the
mid-twentieth century. Open March to November.

PAINSHILL PARK
Portsmouth, Cobham, Surrey KT11 1JE
Tel: 01932 868113
One of the greatest eighteenth-century landscape
gardens. Open all year round. Its impressive rococo
garden, restored since the 1970s, is open January to
November.

PENSHURST PLACE
Penshurst, nr Tonbridge, Kent TN11 8DG
Tel: 01892 870307
Medieval castellated mansion, with formal gardens
restored in the nineteenth and twentieth centuries.
Open April to October.

PETWORTH HOUSE (NT)
Petworth, West Sussex GU28 0AE
Tel: 01798 342207
One of Capability Brown's most celebrated
landscapes. Open March to December.

PLAS NEWYDD (NT)
Llanfairpwll, Anglesey, Wales LL61 6QD
Tel: 01248 714795
Wonderful picturesque garden on the banks of the
Menai Strait. Open March to November.

POWIS CASTLE (NT)
Welshpool, Powys SY21 8RF
Tel: 01938 551929
Spectacular medieval castle with Renaissance and
eighteenth-century gardens. Open March to
October.

QUEEN ELEANOR'S GARDEN
The Great Hall, Winchester, Hampshire SO23 8UL
Tel: 01962 846476
Re-created medieval garden. Open all year round.

ROUSHAM HOUSE
Steeple Aston, Bicester, Oxfordshire OX25 3QX
Tel: 01869 347110
Exquisite eighteenth-century gardens by William
Kent. Open all year round.

SHRUBLAND PARK
Coddenham, Ipswich, Suffolk IP6 9QQ
Tel: 01473 830221
Theatrically terraced Victorian gardens by Sir
Charles Barry. Open April to September.

SISSINGHURST CASTLE GARDEN (NT)
Sissinghurst, nr Cranbrook, Kent TN17 2AB
Tel: 01580 710700
Famous twentieth-century garden developed around
an Elizabethan mansion. Open March to October.

STOURHEAD (NT)
Stourton, Warminster, Wiltshire BA12 6QD
Tel: 01747 841152
Justly celebrated eighteenth-century garden of
artfully contrived views. Open all year round.

STOWE LANDSCAPE GARDENS (NT)
Buckingham, Buckinghamshire MK18 5EH
Tel: 01494 755568/01280 822850
One of the great examples of the English landscape garden. Open all year round.

STUDLEY ROYAL (NT)
Fountains, Ripon, North Yorkshire HG4 3DY
Tel: 01765 608888
Eighteenth-century gardens of extraordinary variety and beauty. Open all year round.

SUDELEY CASTLE
Winchcombe, Cheltenham, Gloucestershire GL54 5JD
Tel: 01242 602308
Nineteenth-century re-creation of earlier formal gardens. Open April to October.

TATTON PARK (NT)
Knutsford, Cheshire WA16 6QN
Tel: 01625 534400
Sumptuous Victorian gardens, including restored kitchen garden and glasshouses. Open all year round.

WADDESDON MANOR (NT)
Waddesdon, nr Aylesbury, Buckinghamshire HP18 0JH
Tel: 01296 653203/653211
Nineteenth-century gardens laid out for the Rothschild family. Open all year round.

WESTBURY COURT (NT)
Westbury-on-Severn, Gloucestershire GL14 1PD
Tel: 01452 760461
Late seventeenth-century formal water gardens. Open March to October.

WEST WYCOMBE PARK (NT)
West Wycombe, Buckinghamshire HP14 3AJ
Tel: 01494 513569
Well-preserved eighteenth-century rococo landscape garden. Open April to August.

WILTON HOUSE
Wilton, Salisbury, Wiltshire SP2 0BJ
Tel: 01722 746720/746729
Palladian house with eighteenth-century gardens and later additions. Open April to October.

WOBURN ABBEY
Woburn, Bedfordshire MK17 9WA
Tel: 01525 290666
A good example of Humphry Repton's work. Open March to September.

WOLLATON HALL AND PARK
Wollaton, Nottinghamshire NG8 2AE
Tel: 01159 153900
Elizabethan house with terraced garden. Open April to September.

WREST PARK
Silsoe, Luton, Bedfordshire MK45 4HS
Tel: 01525 860152
Formal canal and gardens in the late seventeenth-century French style. Open April to September.

INDEX

Page numbers in *italics* refer to illustrations

PICTURE CREDITS

The publishers thank the following photographers for the use of their work: Paul Barker/Country Life Picture Library 6b, 7d, 24, 27, 39, 40, 48, 173, 209, 232, 248, 256; Clive Boursnell/Country Life Picture Library 5, 6a&c, 7b, 12, 34, 52, 65, 66, 87, 97, 147, 156, 164, 170, 180-1, 186, 194, 214, 226, 241, 247, 251; Michael Boys/Country Life Picture Library 22, 104, 117; June Buck/Country Life Picture Library 18, 211; Val Corbett/Country Life Picture Library 43, 57, 79, 92, 98, 99r, 114, 120, 122, 132, 139, 140, 153, 160, 185, 220, 224, 224; Julian Easten/Country Life Picture Library 85; Andrew Eburne 3, 7e, 80, 112, 205, 212, 231, 241, 253, 254, 260; J.M. Gibson/Country Life Picture Library 23, 199, 235, 238; Jerry Harpur/Country Life Picture Library 128; Marcus Harpur/Country Life Picture Library 219, 240; Sannina Hartell/Country Life Picture Library 97; Anne Hyde/Country Life Picture Library 6d, 10, 47, 90, 110, 126, 210; Tim Imrie-Tait 58, 69, 143; Andrew Lawson/Country Life Picture Library 124; Julian Nieman/Country Life Picture Archive 7c, 202; Hugh Palmer/Country Life Picture Library 76, 223; Alex Ramsey/Country Life Picture Library 33, 56, 84, 95, 135, 217, 234; Nicola Stocken Tompkins/Country Life Picture Library 7a, 99, 136, 148; Sue Witney/Country Life Picture Library 60-1; Steve Wooster/Country Life Picture Library 44, 71.

Illustrations on pages 8, 15, 30, 101, 102, 103, 108, 113, 174, 175, 176, 188, 190, 201, 206, 215, 255, 257, and 261 from *The Gardener's Assistant* by Robert Thompson (London, 1878); 13, 21, 29b, 36, 51, 53, 59, 63, 75, 77, 109, 129, 130, 131, 134, 137, 150, 159, 203, 230 and 237 from *Medieval Gardens* Vols. 1 and 2 by Sir Frank Crisp (London, 1924); 16, 29t, 31, 32, 41, 54, 73, 89, 172 and 178 from *A History of Garden Art* Vols. 1 and 2, ed. Walter P. Wright (London, 1928); 164 from *Oxford's College Gardens* by Eleanour Sinclair Rohde (London, 1932).

ACKNOWLEDGEMENTS

Amongst many debts of gratitude are those due to Tim Mowl, Kate Felus, and John Phibbs for their advice and formidable garden scholarship; to Carey Smith, Sarah Lavelle, Trish Burgess, David Fordham and Natalie Hunt at Random House; and to Michael Gearin-Tosh and John Bayley, for a first introduction to the delights of the English language, at St Catherine's College, Oxford, twenty years ago.